P9-DBS-735

THE GREAT BIBLE QUESTION & ANSWER BOOK

From the Old and New Testaments

Illustrated by Gonzales Vicente

Written by Claudia Vurnakes

Published by Playmore Inc., Publishers, 58 Main Street, Hackensack, N.J. 07601

Printed in the U.S.A.

TO THE PARENT

THE GREAT BIBLE QUESTION AND ANSWER BOOK is written clearly in a question and answer format that will help create interest in the Scriptures for young readers. This beautifully illustrated book can serve as an introduction to Bible study or as a learning experience on its own.

All of the well-known figures and events are included, as well as other important points of interest. We hope that you and your child will read this book again and again, while each time finding renewed faith and wonder among its pages.

The Playmore Logo® is a registered trademark of
Playmore Inc., Publishers, Hackensack, N.J.

Copyright © MMVIII Playmore Inc., Publishers

All rights reserved. No part of this book may be reproduced in any form or any media without the express written permission of the publisher.

How did God create the heavens and the earth?

People have wondered about this question as long as human beings have lived on the face of the earth. The Bible tells us that in the beginning, nothing existed but God. He spoke, and the power of His words filled the great emptiness with light, stars, water, and land. He created the sun and the moon to give light and to measure time. Next, He made birds and fish and land animals to multiply and fill the earth with life. God looked on His work and saw that it was good, but He was not finished yet. His last and most important work was creating the first human beings, Adam and Eve.

Why is the Sabbath a day of holy rest?

The word "Sabbath" means "to stop." It stands for the seventh day of Creation when God stopped and rested from His work. The Book of Genesis says that God blessed the Sabbath and made it holy.

From earliest Bible times, people have used the Sabbath as a break from their work and to gather together for worship. The Jewish Sabbath falls on Saturday, the seventh day of the week, while Christians' holy day is Sunday.

In whose image were Adam and Eve created?

According to Genesis, God made Adam from the dust of the earth. While Adam slept, God took a rib from his side and shaped the body of Eve. To both, God gave a breath of His own life. This made Adam and Eve much more than living bodies; it gave them God's very own spirit. Because of this, Adam and Eve could think for themselves. They were not ruled by instinct like the animals. God put the first man and the first woman in charge of the rest of Creation and gave them a beautiful place to live, the Garden of Eden.

What two important trees stood in the Garden of Eden?

The place where Adam and Eve lived was filled with every kind of delicious and satisfying fruit. In the very center stood the Tree of Knowledge and the Tree of Life. The Tree of Knowledge held the understanding of all things, both good and evil. The Tree of Life held eternal life.

God told Adam and Eve they could eat anything in the garden they desired, except for the fruit from the Tree of Knowledge. If they ate this fruit, they would know good and evil, God said, and they would surely die.

5.) How did the serpent tempt Eve in the Garden of Eden?

Living in the garden was an evil spirit who took on the shape of a snake. This serpent asked Eve why God would not allow her to taste the fruit from the Tree of Knowledge. "Eat of the fruit," the snake said, "and you will become just like God! You will have knowledge and power to do anything you please."

Eve saw that the fruit was beautiful, and she wanted to be wise, so she picked the fruit and tasted it. Then she took the fruit to Adam and he also ate it.

6.) What excuse did Adam and Eve make for eating the forbidden fruit?

When Adam and Eve heard the Lord walking in the garden that evening, they hid from Him. But God called to Adam, and asked what he had done. Adam blamed Eve: "The woman gave me the fruit from the Tree of Knowledge, so I ate it." Eve told God that the snake had tricked her.

God punished all three for their sin. To the serpent He said, "From now on, you will crawl on the ground, and people everywhere will curse you." God told Adam and Eve that they would have to leave the Garden of Eden.

7.)

How did Adam and Eve first clothe themselves?

When God created Adam and Eve, they were naked. They were not ashamed of their nakedness because they had no knowledge of good and evil. As soon as Adam and Eve tasted the fruit offered by the serpent, the fruit that God had forbidden them to eat, it was as if their eyes were opened. Now they wanted to hide their bodies, and they wove fig leaves together to cover themselves.

Later, when the Lord sent them from Eden, He killed animals to provide skins for their clothing. This was the first example of sacrifice in the Bible. To cover Adam and Eve's sin, it was necessary to shed an animal's blood.

8.)

How did human life change because Adam and Eve sinned?

Once Adam and Eve chose to eat the fruit from the Tree of Knowledge, life on earth changed forever. In sorrow, God sent his disobedient children out of Eden: "You must leave this perfect life I made for you. Out in the wilderness you will learn about hard work and pain. You will grow old and die because of your disobedience. From now on, every human being will be tempted to sin, and the evil spirit of the serpent will be your enemy. But I make a promise to give you hope. Some day, one of your descendants will crush the serpent's head and destroy evil forever."

Why did Cain kill his brother Abel?

Adam and Eve had two sons after they left the Garden of Eden. Cain was a farmer, and Abel tended animals. The two brothers decided to make an offering to the Lord, so Cain brought some food he had grown and Abel brought a young lamb. They burned their offerings so the smoke would rise to Heaven.

God wanted to teach His people how to worship Him. He told the brothers that grain gathered from the land was not a pleasing gift. The Lord required that the lifeblood of an animal be shed as an offering. Abel's gift pleased God; Cain's did not.

This made Cain furious, but God said, "Don't be angry, Cain. I will be pleased with you when you make a right offering."

Cain could not get over his anger. He went out in the field and killed his brother.

Later God asked Cain, "Where is Abel?"

"Am I my brother's keeper? I do not know." Cain replied.

But God knew what Cain had done. He placed a mark on Cain's forehead and took away his ability to grow crops. In shame and sorrow, Cain left his home and went to the land of Nod. There he married and began building a city.

10.)

Who were the Nephilim?

The Book of Genesis describes the Nephilim as a race of giant warriors, the children of earthly women and heavenly angels. Later in the Old Testament, when Joshua sent spies to the Promised Land, they returned with more stories about the Nephilim: "Those people are very tall and strong. We look like grasshoppers beside them. It is impossible to defeat them in battle."

In spite of these reports about the huge Nephilim people, Joshua and his men succeeded in capturing the Promised Land.

11.)

Why did God send the Great Flood to cover the earth?

In the years after Adam and Eve left the Garden of Eden, the human race grew and filled the earth. People built towns; they planted crops and tended sheep. But they also did evil things to one another. God saw violence everywhere and He was sorry that He had created human beings. "I will destroy everything on the face of the earth," He said. "Every human, every animal, every bird."

But there was one good man — Noah. God decided to save Noah and his family, and He told them about the flood that would come. He gave them instructions for building an ark, a large boat that would keep them safe in the days of the flood.

How big was the ark that Noah built?

God told Noah to build a boat 300 cubits long. A cubit is the distance from an adult's fingertips to his elbow, about 18 inches. That means that the ark was 450 feet, an enormous boat. The ark would need a huge ocean, but there was no water anywhere near Noah's home.

Noah did not question God. He built the boat as the Lord directed, with one window, one door, and rooms on three floors. Noah was to fill the rooms with every kind of food for the animals that God would bring to the door of the ark.

How long did Noah and the animals stay in the ark?

When two of every kind of animal had come, The Lord Himself closed the door and the storms began. For 40 days it rained and floods washed over the highest peaks for the next 150 days. It took another 150 days for the water to begin to go down. By the first day of the tenth month, the tops of the mountains showed. Noah waited 40 days and then sent out a dove. When the bird could not find a dry place to land, Noah knew it was not yet time to leave the ark. Two weeks later, the dove did not return. Noah opened the door and released the animals, after spending more than a year inside the boat.

14.) Where did Noah's ark come to rest on land?

According to the story in Genesis, when the waters of the Great Flood began to settle, the ark stopped on top of Mount Ararat. This peak is located in a mountainous region far to the northeast, what is now the nation of Turkey. The land there is extremely good. As Noah and his family left the ark to build new lives, they found rich pastures for their herds and fertile soil for crops. God brought them to a place where beginning again would be easy.

15.) What promise did God make about the rainbow?

After all the flood waters dried up, Noah released the animals from the ark and offered a sacrifice to God. This pleased the Lord, and he promised Noah that never again would He send water to destroy every living thing on the earth. God told Noah and his family that the rainbow would be a sign of this promise. Whenever rain clouds filled the sky and colors bridged the heavens, God would remember his covenant: that as long as the earth continued, there would never be another Great Flood.

Where did Noah's descendants live?

After the Flood, God told the families of Noah's three sons, Shem, Ham, and Japheth, to have many children. The families grew and became different nations, spreading out to fill Asia, Africa and the world.

One of Noah's descendants was the great hunter Nimrod. He became the ruler of the kingdom of Babel, and for many generations, people remembered Nimrod's great power.

What did the builders of the Tower of Babel hope to do?

The kingdom of Babel prospered and the people learned to make bricks. They saw how easy it was to build things, and they felt very smart indeed.

"Let us make a tower that will reach all the way to Heaven. We will be famous, and everyone will fear us!"

These thoughts displeased the Lord. "The people all speak one language and they feel as smart as gods. I will give them different languages so they will not be able to talk to each other."

Instantly, work on the tower stopped. No one could understand the words of the person next to him. Because of this, the people split up and went to live with those who spoke the same language.

Who was Abraham?

Of all the people in the Bible, Abraham is the person best known for his great faith in God. Abraham followed the Lord's leading and moved from Ur to Canaan, where he became the father of the Hebrew nation.

But Abraham did not always worship the Lord, and his name was not always Abraham. He was born Abram, the son of Terah, a man who made idols. In those days, the people worshipped many gods, and they made statues of them. They thought these statues had supernatural powers. But Abram heard the voice of the One True God, who told him to leave the land of the idol-worshippers.

Abram worshipped God instead of bowing to the idols of his fathers. Because of Abram's great faith, God changed his name to Abraham, which means "father of many nations." Through Abraham's descendants, knowledge of the One True God spread throughout the world.

What is a covenant?

A covenant is a special agreement, an important promise. All through the Bible, God made covenants with His people, like His promise to Abraham. Before Abraham ever had a child, God promised that his family would grow into a great nation. On his part, Abraham promised to worship no other god but the Lord.

Who was Ishmael?

God promised Abraham many descendants, but years went by and Abraham and his wife Sarah had no children. So Abraham decided not to wait on the Lord any longer. He had a son with Sarah's servant Hagar when he was 86 years old. Hagar named the boy Ishmael.

Later, when Sarah had a son of her own, she insisted that Ishmael and his mother leave Abraham's tents. They were sent out in the desert, and Hagar feared they would die. But God promised to be with Ishmael. The boy grew up in the desert and learned to be an expert shot with a bow. His descendants became a large tribe of people known as the Ishmaelites who lived in the wilderness of Arabia.

Why did Sarah laugh at God's message?

After many years of longing for a child, Sarah grew old. When she was 90 years old, angels visited Abraham and told him Sarah would finally have a son. When Sarah heard the news, she laughed. "It's impossible! I am much too old to have a baby!"

But God did what He promised. Sarah had a son, and she named him Isaac, which means "laughter." Sarah said, "In my old age, God has made me laugh for joy!"

How did God use Isaac to test Abraham?

After waiting so many years to have a son, Abraham loved Isaac dearly. One day, God spoke to Abraham. "Take Isaac up to a mountaintop and give the boy to me as a burnt offering."

This command brought tears to Abraham's eyes, but he knew he must obey the Lord. So he chopped some firewood and started up the mountain with his beloved son.

Isaac watched his father build an altar. Fear and bewilderment filled the boy's heart as Abraham tied Isaac's hands and lifted him up on the stone table. Abraham reached for the knife to kill his son.

At that moment, God called to Abraham. "Let the boy go. Now I know that you truly respect Me. You were willing to give me your only son Isaac."

What is an altar?

An altar is a place where sacrifices, gifts and prayers were given to God. The first altars in the Bible were just piles of stones. People built altars and gave sacrifices anywhere they felt close to God - on a mountaintop, at a battle-field, or where they had received a special blessing.

Later, when the Temple was built in Jerusalem, the altar was made of rare wood decorated with gold. It was the priests' job to place the offerings to the Lord on the altar.

How did Abraham find the bride God intended for Isaac?

Isaac grew up in Canaan, in the land where God had led Abraham. Soon it was time for the young man to marry, but Abraham did not want his son to choose a Canaanite woman: They worshipped pagan gods. So Abraham sent a faithful servant back to his homeland to find a wife among Abraham's own people.

As the servant neared the gates of Abraham's old city, he worried about his task. "What if no young woman will return with me?" He prayed that God would show him the right bride for Isaac.

Before he had even finished this prayer, a beautiful girl came to the well outside the city gates. She kindly offered the servant water for his camels. The servant learned the young woman, named Rebekah, was from a family related to Abraham. "Clearly, this is from the Lord, the God of my master! He had led me to the bride for Isaac."

Rebekah's family gave their blessing, and the two returned to Canaan. From a long way off, Isaac watched them coming. He married Rebekah and loved her very much.

What was Esau's birthright?

Twin sons, Jacob and Esau, were born to Isaac and Rebekah. As the boys grew, Esau, the older of the twins, loved to hunt wild animals. The younger twin, Jacob, quietly tended the sheep. One day Esau returned from a hunting trip with a great hunger. He smelled the pottage Jacob had cooked for himself, and Esau wanted it.

"I'll give you some stew," Jacob said. "But first, you must give me your birthright."

As the older son, someday Esau would inherit all of Isaac's flocks. But that seemed a long way off to Esau. He wanted food right away, so he traded all his inheritance for a dish of pottage.

What foods did people eat in Bible times?

Most Hebrew families ate two meals a day. Breakfast was flat bread, a piece of cheese, and some dried fruit or olives. There was no noon meal, but families sometimes had something to drink or pieces of fruit.

Dinner consisted of stew, called pottage, made from fresh vegetables or dried lentils. Only on special occasions was meat or fish added to the pot. Family members used pieces of bread to scoop up the stew, as there was no silverware. At the end of the meal, fruit and wine were served.

How did Jacob trick Isaac?

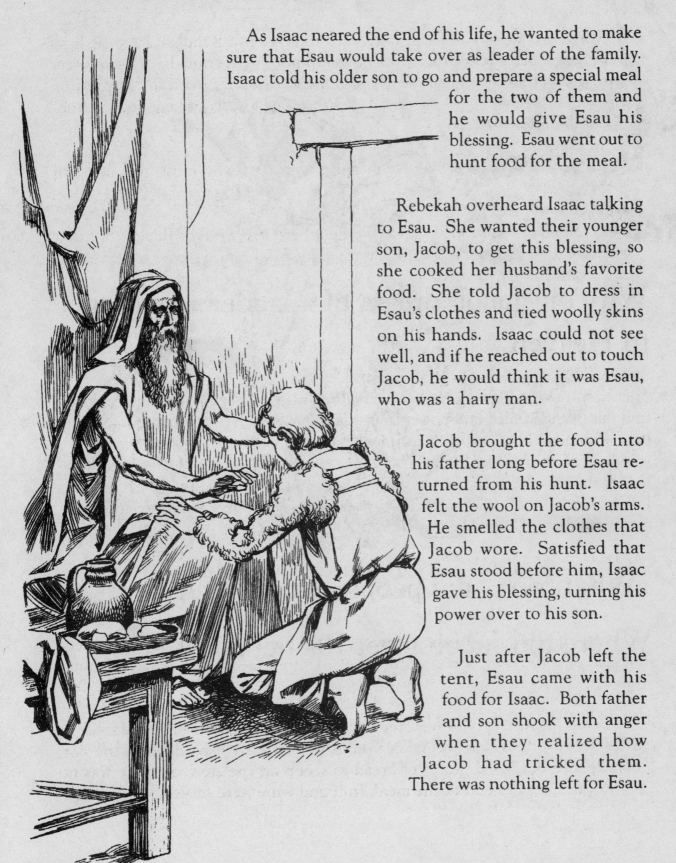

As Isaac neared the end of his life, he wanted to make sure that Esau would take over as leader of the family. Isaac told his older son to go and prepare a special meal for the two of them and he would give Esau his blessing. Esau went out to hunt food for the meal.

Rebekah overheard Isaac talking to Esau. She wanted their younger son, Jacob, to get this blessing, so she cooked her husband's favorite food. She told Jacob to dress in Esau's clothes and tied woolly skins on his hands. Isaac could not see well, and if he reached out to touch Jacob, he would think it was Esau, who was a hairy man.

Jacob brought the food into his father long before Esau returned from his hunt. Isaac felt the wool on Jacob's arms. He smelled the clothes that Jacob wore. Satisfied that Esau stood before him, Isaac gave his blessing, turning his power over to his son.

Just after Jacob left the tent, Esau came with his food for Isaac. Both father and son shook with anger when they realized how Jacob had tricked them. There was nothing left for Esau.

Why did Jacob dream of a ladder reaching to Heaven?

Esau wanted to kill Jacob when he realized his younger brother had tricked him out of the wealth and power that should have been his. Jacob ran for his life. Alone out in the wilderness, Jacob had plenty of time to think about the way he had mistreated Esau. The young man fell asleep and dreamed of a ladder that reached to Heaven, with angels coming and going. In his dream Jacob heard a voice, "I am the Lord your God. I will give you this land and many children. Do not be afraid, for I am with you."

Jacob awoke with courage and hope in his heart. He decided to put his dishonest deeds behind him and go wherever the Lord might lead him.

Where did Jacob meet Rachel and Leah?

Jacob traveled to the land of Aram where his uncle Laban lived. When he greeted his relatives, he saw a beautiful girl watering her flocks. It was Rachel. Jacob promised to work seven years for Laban if he could marry Rachel. Laban tricked Jacob and on the wedding night gave him Leah, Rachel's older sister. Now Jacob knew what it felt like to be tricked. But he still wanted Rachel for his wife, so he worked another seven years for Laban.

Why did Jacob wrestle with an angel?

After Jacob had lived with his uncle Laban for twenty years, God told him to go back to the land of Canaan. So Jacob packed his tents and gathered his family to make the journey home. As he traveled with his large flocks, Jacob had plenty of time to remember the evil things he had done to his brother.

One night as Jacob rested by a stream, an angel grabbed him, and they wrestled back and forth until the sun came up. No matter how hard the angel tried, he could not defeat Jacob. "I will not let you go," Jacob said, "until you bless me!"

The angel blessed Jacob and gave him a new name, Israel. In Hebrew, this name means, "he wrestles with God."

When did Jacob and Esau put their angry past behind them?

After his struggle with the angel, Jacob crossed the stream that flowed by his homeland. Soon, he saw Esau coming to meet him. Four hundred men traveled with Esau, and Jacob trembled in fear. But Esau ran to his brother. He hugged him and cried tears of joy. The brothers exchanged many gifts, and from that day on, lived in peace with one another.

What gift did Israel give his favorite son?

Twelve sons were born to Jacob, who was now known as Israel. Joseph, born when Israel was an old man, became his father's favorite. When Joseph grew so much that he needed a new coat, his father had one made of the finest cloth money could buy. The coat had long sleeves and stripes of many colors – red, blue, purple. It was a coat fit for a prince. None of Joseph's older brothers had ever worn a coat like this one, and they were jealous of their younger brother.

Why did Joseph's dreams upset his brothers?

It was bad enough that of all twelve sons, Israel loved Joseph the most. But when Joseph began talking about his strange dreams, the brothers grew very angry.

"I dreamed we were all stacks of wheat," Joseph said. "Your stacks bowed down to my stack." Another time the young boy dreamed that even the sun, the moon, and the stars bowed before him.

Finally, the brothers could stand it no longer. They made a plan to kill the young dreamer. But a band of traders passed nearby, so the brothers sold Joseph instead. They smeared animal blood on the fancy coat and took it home to Israel. The old man cried because he thought his favorite son was dead.

Why was Joseph thrown in prison?

When the traders who bought Joseph arrived in Egypt, they sold him as a slave. The young Hebrew worked for a man named Potiphar, and tried to honor the Lord in all that he did. Potiphar saw Joseph's good work and placed him in charge of the entire household.

Joseph was a handsome man, and Potiphar's wife desired him. Even though Joseph ran from her, she lied and told Potiphar that the slave had tried to attack her. Joseph was arrested and spent two years in prison for something he did not do. But the Lord continued to be with Joseph. The jailer put the young man in charge of the other prisoners.

Why was Joseph able to explain dreams?

This was in the time that Pharaoh ruled in Egypt. While Joseph was in jail, two of Pharaoh's officers, his butler and baker, were arrested and sent to the same prison. Both men had troubling dreams and went to Joseph.

"God is the only one who can give you answers," Joseph said. After listening carefully, he told them the meaning of their dreams. One man, the baker, would die. The other man, the butler, would live to serve Pharaoh again. When the dreams came true exactly as Joseph said, everyone in the prison was amazed.

Why did Pharaoh dream of cows and corn?

While Joseph was in prison, Pharaoh had two dreams that puzzled him. In his first dream he saw seven fat cows eating grass. Seven thin cows came and ate up the fat ones. In the second dream, seven thin ears of corn ate up seven full ears. None of Pharaoh's advisors knew what the dreams meant. The butler remembered Joseph's great ability, so Pharaoh summoned the young man.

Joseph explained that the seven fat cows and seven full ears of corn stood for seven years of plenty. They would be followed by seven years of hunger. Joseph said that Pharaoh should store up food so his people would not starve during the seven lean years.

How did Joseph save all of Egypt from starvation?

When Joseph suggested that Egypt should start saving food for the seven lean years that were to come, Pharaoh saw that Joseph was very wise. He put the young man in charge of building huge storehouses and collecting grain from the people. For seven years, crops grew well, and Joseph set aside much food. But the time came when nothing would grow. People ate the last of their own grain and would have starved, but Joseph opened the storehouses and fed the people.

What happened when Joseph's brothers came to buy grain?

Except for Pharaoh, Joseph was the most powerful man in all of Egypt. He wore clothes of fine linen and a gold chain around his neck. When he rode in his chariot, people who had come from distant countries to buy food bowed before him.

Over in the land of Canaan, Israel's family had also run out of grain. When the old man heard that Egypt had food to sell, he sent his ten older sons to buy some. Joseph knew his brothers the minute they came to the palace. They only saw a powerful Egyptian officer.

How did all twelve sons of Israel come to live in Egypt?

When Joseph saw his older brothers, he decided to trick them. "You are spies!" he said. "I will not sell you any more grain until you bring your youngest brother to me. That way I will know you are honest men."

The brothers returned to Egypt with Benjamin, the youngest son, and Joseph burst into tears. "I am your brother Joseph!" he told them. "You sold me as a slave, but God used me to save people's lives here in Egypt."

The brothers hugged and kissed each other. Joseph sent them back to Canaan to get their father and their families. When the old man, Israel, saw Joseph, he cried, "Now I can die in peace, for I have seen my son Joseph once more!"

Why did Pharaoh order the Hebrews' baby boys put to death?

After Joseph brought his brothers to live in Egypt, the family prospered and many children were born. The years passed, and Joseph died. A new Pharaoh sat on the throne of Egypt. He saw that the family of Israel had grown into a strong large tribe. So he ordered that the Hebrews work as the Egyptians' slaves, building new cities and growing grain.

But Pharaoh still was not satisfied. Worried that the Hebrews continued to have too many healthy children, he decided to have their baby boys drowned in the river.

How was baby Moses rescued?

When Pharaoh ordered all the Hebrew baby boys put to death, Moses' mother thought of a plan that might save her infant son. She made a waterproof basket, placed the baby inside, and floated the basket in the Nile River. Her hope was that someone would find the child and keep him.

Someone did -- Pharaoh's daughter. When she went to the river to bathe, she saw the basket and had it brought to her. She adopted the baby as her own child and named him Moses, which means "pulled from the water."

What kind of education did Moses receive?

The Bible tells us that Moses grew up in the palace of Pharaoh. No other facts about his childhood are given, but as the son of Pharaoh's daughter, Moses probably would have had the best teachers in all of Egypt. He may have read scrolls from one of the world's greatest libraries, for the Pharaohs had collected thousands of books on medicine, science, religion, history and magic. Egypt was a center of business. People brought unusual things from distant lands to sell at the marketplaces. Moses must have seen and heard things most other young men could only dream about. It was an education fit for a prince.

Why did Moses flee from Pharaoh's court?

As Moses grew to manhood in the palace of Pharaoh, he learned that he had been adopted as a baby. He was not the son of an Egyptian princess, he was a Jew. Moses went out where the Jewish slaves were working and saw an Egyptian master whip a man. In anger, Moses killed the Egyptian. He realized he would be punished for this crime if he remained at Pharaoh's court, so he fled into the wilderness.

Who was Jethro?

After Moses killed the Egyptian slave master, he ran from Egypt into the desert of Midian. For days, he wandered alone in the wilderness, seeking shelter from the scorching sun. At last, Moses stumbled upon a well. As he drank, a family of young women brought their sheep to the well for water. Soon other shepherds arrived with their flocks and tried to push the sisters away. Moses protected the young women, who invited him to come and live with their father, Jethro. Jethro welcomed Moses to his tents and trusted him with his flocks. The older man was a priest of the Lord, and probably taught Moses much about the God of his fathers. Moses later married one of Jethro's daughters, Zipporah, and had two sons.

How long did Moses live as a shepherd?

Moses stayed in the desert for many years, tending sheep. He probably thought his life as an Egyptian prince was long in the past. But God had other plans. The old Pharaoh died; a new one took his place. Life for the Hebrew slaves grew even harder under the new Pharaoh, and they cried to the Lord for help. God heard their cries and remembered His promises to Abraham, Isaac, and Jacob. After Moses' time in the wilderness, God was ready to send him back to Egypt.

What happened at the burning bush?

One day Moses was out with his flocks near Mount Sinai, the place where the people of Midian went to worship God. There he saw a bush covered in flames, but the fire did not destroy the bush. As Moses stared in amazement, the Lord spoke from the center of the flame. "Moses, I am sending you to Pharaoh. Go! Bring My people out of Egypt!"

But Moses said to God, "I am not a great king. Why should Pharaoh listen to me?"

God told Moses to throw his walking stick on the ground. As Moses watched, the stick became a snake. Next, God covered Moses' hand with a bad skin disease and immediately healed it. "Go back to Egypt, Moses," God said. "I will give you powers like these so Pharaoh will listen."

Who was Aaron?

Aaron was Moses' brother and the first high priest of Israel.

When God instructed Moses to ask Pharaoh to release the Hebrew people, Moses protested that he was not good at speaking. God told Moses to bring his brother Aaron with him to Pharaoh's court. Aaron was a skilled speaker and announced to Pharaoh all the messages God gave Moses. When the people left Egypt, the Lord chose Aaron and his sons to serve as priests. Aaron died before the people reached the Promised Land.

How did God convince Pharaoh to let the Hebrews go?

Moses and his brother Aaron went before Pharaoh and asked him to free the Hebrew slaves so they could go back to their homeland. But Pharaoh just laughed and made the people work even harder. God told Moses He would send ten plagues to punish all of Egypt and then, at last, Pharaoh would let the people go.

For the first plague, Moses turned all the water in Egypt to blood. Next, God sent a plague of frogs that jumped into every kitchen, every bed, even Pharaoh's palace. The third plague was a huge swarm of gnats, but still Pharaoh would not let the Hebrews go.

A plague of flies, a plague of animal disease, and a plague of sores on people's bodies only made Pharaoh more stubborn. The seventh plague was hail that destroyed crops and killed animals. Next, the Lord sent locusts which ate everything left from the hailstorm, and darkness covered the land for three days. Pharaoh said to Moses, "I'm tired of these plagues. Do not come back or I will kill you."

So Moses did not go back to Pharaoh's court. Instead he sent a message from God. "Tonight, I, the Lord, will pass through the land. Every firstborn son in Egypt will die. And at last you will let My people go."

What happened at the first Passover?

Pharaoh did not believe that the God of Israel had the power to cause every firstborn child in the land of Egypt to die. But the Hebrews did. They carefully followed these instructions from God. "Sacrifice a lamb and mark your door with its blood. Then when I come through Egypt tonight, I will pass over your house. In every unmarked house, a child shall die, and there will be crying in all the land. But the Egyptians will see that you are My people, and they will let you go."

And it happened just as God promised.

Why did the Hebrews have to eat unleavened bread?

When the Egyptians discovered that their oldest children had died, they feared the God of Moses. "Go now!" they told the Hebrew slaves. "Take all of your sheep and cattle. Hurry, before your God sets another terrible plague upon us!"

So the Hebrew people left quickly, taking only what they could carry with them. Mothers rushed to prepare food for the journey, wrapping up bread dough before it was ready for yeast. The people marched into the wilderness, and they used the unleavened dough they had brought with them for bread. Without yeast, the bread baked hard and flat.

From that day until now, the Jews eat unleavened bread at Passover, to remember the people's great rush to leave Egypt.

How did the Israelites cross the Red Sea?

The Hebrew people marched out of Egypt and stopped to camp on the shore of the Red Sea. They were free at last! Soon, though, the sound of rumbling chariots filled their hearts with fear. Pharaoh had changed his mind. His soldiers came with spears and swords to bring the slaves back to Egypt. But God did not forget His people. Moses raised his stick and the waves moved back, leaving a dry path right through the middle of the Red Sea. The people crossed safely to the other side. Pharaoh's army tried to follow, but God rolled the waters back and all the soldiers drowned.

Who was Miriam?

How the Hebrews rejoiced when they saw Pharaoh's army drown in the sea! Moses' sister, Miriam, led the people in worshipping God. Playing her tambourine, she sang, "The Lord is worthy of great honor! Sing to Him! He has thrown the horse and rider into the sea!"

Moses must have loved Miriam very much. When she had been a young girl, she had guarded her baby brother's basket as it floated in the river. As a grown woman, she still helped Moses, showing the people how to honor God in the wilderness.

How did the Lord provide food for the people in the wilderness?

The Israelites had seen that God's words were true; He had brought them safely out of Egypt just as He had promised. But now in the wilderness they grumbled and complained that there was no food or water. Had God forgotten them?

The Lord answered their grumblings. He commanded Moses to strike a rock with his stick. Water enough for all poured from the rock. Then He gave Moses a message for the people: "Every evening, you will have meat. And every morning you can have all the bread you want. Then you will know I am the Lord, your God."

At night, small birds covered the ground. The people caught them and cooked them for their meal. In the morning, the desert was white with thin flakes. The people named this delicious bread from heaven "manna."

Every day, the Israelites caught birds at night, and woke up to find manna for breakfast. On the morning of the sixth day, Moses told the people to gather twice as much as they needed, for there would be no food found on the seventh day. God wanted His children to learn to keep the Sabbath.

Why did God give Moses the Ten Commandments?

Three months after the Israelites left Egypt, they reached the foot of Mount Sinai. Moses climbed up the mountain and God spoke to him there. "Tell the people to listen. I am going to give them special laws so they will always be My holy people."

The Israelites carefully washed their clothes and their bodies so they would be clean before the Lord. Moses went back up Mount Sinai and stayed for forty days and nights. During that time, the earth shook. Clouds of fire appeared around the mountain. God gave Moses his laws for living and carved them on tablets of stone. When Moses took the tablets down the mountain, his face shone so with the glory of the Lord that the people were afraid to look at him.

What rules for living are covered by the Ten Commandments?

God gave the Hebrew people ten laws that taught them how to live as His holy people. The first four laws showed them how to live with God. The next six laws taught about getting along with other people.

1. I am the Lord your God. You must have no other god but Me.
2. You must not make any graven images.
3. You must not use My name carelessly.
4. Remember the Sabbath, My holy day.
5. Honor your mother and your father.
6. You must not kill.
7. You must be faithful in marriage.
8. You must not steal.
9. You must not tell lies.
10. You must not desire things that belong to your neighbor.

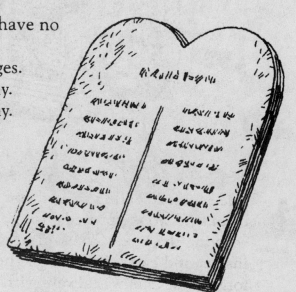

Why did the people worship a golden calf in the wilderness?

Moses stayed up on Mount Sinai talking to God for forty days and forty nights. The people saw the lightning on the mountaintop; they heard the thunder and felt the earth move. They were afraid. They thought Moses would never return. So they went to Aaron, Moses' brother. "Make us another god who will lead us out of this wilderness."

Aaron collected gold earrings from the people. He melted them down and made a statue of a calf. When Moses came down the mountain, he found the people worshipping at the feet of the golden statue.

What is the Ark of the Covenant?

When Moses saw that his people had forgotten the one true God, he threw the stone tablets of the Ten Commandments on the ground. They shattered into bits. "Forgive us, God!" he prayed. "Don't be angry with these foolish people! Remember your promises to Abraham, Isaac, and Jacob."

So the Lord had mercy on the Israelites. He gave Moses another set of tablets listing His commands. And to help the people honor these laws, God told Moses to build a special box. This was the Ark of the Covenant. It was to be of fine wood covered with gold. There were to be poles on each side for carrying the box. God said to place the tablets of the Ten Commandments inside, and carry it wherever the people went. That way they would never forget that God was always with them.

What did Moses' spies report about the Promised Land?

All twelve men chosen to spy on the land of Canaan returned to Moses with good news about the crops. They showed the people huge grapes, figs and pomegranates they had picked there. But they also told of the strong walled cities they saw. "We can not attack those people," the spies said. "They are too strong for us. We should return to Egypt."

Only two spies, Joshua and Caleb, believed the people should march into Canaan. "Do not fear the enemy tribes," they said. "If the Lord is pleased with us, He will give us this land."

Why did it take 40 years to reach the Promised Land?

No matter how the Lord had cared for the Israelites in the wilderness, they had complained. They had worried about finding water to drink and having bread and meat for meals. They had feared snakes in the desert and now they feared the enemy tribes living in Canaan. After coming all the way from Egypt, they wanted to turn back.

At last God grew angry. "How long will these people grumble? As surely as My glory fills the earth, I make this promise: not one adult among you who has complained will enter the Promised Land. You will wander in the wilderness for forty years and die there because you have tested Me so many times. Only the children among you will get to see the Promised Land."

What did Zelophehad's daughters request?

Zelophehad was one of the Hebrew men who left Egypt with Moses. He died in the wilderness, and his daughters worried they would have no home when they entered the Promised Land. At that time, women were not allowed to own property. But Zelophehad's daughters bravely went to Moses and asked for their father's share of land. Because of these young women, the Lord gave Moses a new law. From that time on, daughters could inherit their fathers' property.

What did Moses see from Mount Nebo?

At last, the Israelites' long years of wandering neared an end. God told Moses soon it would be his time to die. Even though Moses was a man of great faith, there had once been a time when even he had doubted God would take care of the people. For this sin, God could not allow Moses to enter the Promised Land.

Instead, God told Moses to go to Mount Nebo. There, he could look down on the land of Canaan with its fruitful plains, palm trees and valleys. With the beautiful sight of the Promised Land before him, Moses died. The Lord Himself buried this great leader, and to this day, no one knows exactly where his grave is located.

Who led the Hebrew people into the Promised Land?

Joshua was a general in Moses' army. He led the people in battle against enemy tribes, and he visited the Promised Land as one of Moses' spies. Of the twelve men who saw Canaan, only Joshua and Caleb believed God would give them the land. So forty years later, God chose Joshua to lead the people into the Promised Land. Filled with wisdom from the Lord, Joshua and his army captured cities and divided them fairly among the Israelite families.

What kind of country was the Promised Land?

Before his death, Moses had told the people all about the land which God would one day give them. "It is a good land, a land of milk and honey. Wheat, figs and olives are plentiful. Your herds will grow large there, and you will have much silver and gold."

The Israelites carried this hope in their hearts for forty years. When at last Joshua led them across the Jordan River into the land of Canaan, they saw their dreams come true. The Promised Land was indeed a rich land, flowing with milk and honey.

What was the Tabernacle?

The Tabernacle was the holy tent where God met His people in worship, from the time of Moses until the Great Temple was built in Jerusalem. The Lord commanded that the finest materials be used in making this tent: gold, silver, bronze, red and purple cloth, soft leather, spices, rubies, sapphires and topaz. The Tabernacle was indeed an awesome sight.

A large courtyard constructed of linen curtains surrounded the tent. In this court stood an altar for burnt offerings and a large basin where the priests washed their hands.

The most important place was the tent itself. It had a wooden frame and was covered with soft animal skins. Inside, the walls were hung with rich tapestries and a veil divided the space in half. In front of the veil stood a table where offering bread was placed. Behind the veil was the Ark of the Covenant, the gold-covered box in which the Ten Commandments were stored.

The Israelites took the Tabernacle with them wherever they went. It was a reminder that God was always with them.

Where did the Tabernacle stay during the time of the judges?

When the Israelites entered the Promised Land, they selected a permanent spot for the Tabernacle, a place called Shiloh. Throughout Joshua's life and during the time that followed, when judges ruled the land, Shiloh served as Israel's religious center. Families visited the Tabernacle every year to worship and make offerings to the Lord.

What is the Shofar?

The Shofar is a musical instrument made from a ram's horn. It was used in the Tabernacle and later in the Great Temple. Moses blew on the first Shofar to call the people together in the wilderness. It announced the Sabbath, warned of danger, signaled in battle, or proclaimed a new leader. The Shofar is the only instrument from the early days of Israel to still be used in synagogues today.

What is the Day of Atonement?

From the time of Moses, the Jewish people have observed the Day of Atonement. It is the time they ask God to forgive the sins of all the people. During Old Testament years, the high priest sacrificed one goat as an offering to the Lord. He would send another goat out into the wilderness to show that the people's sins were sent far away. On this most holy day of the year, people stop their work and go without food so they can spend the entire time praying to the Lord.

What promise did Hannah make to God?

During the time of the judges, there was a woman named Hannah who did not have any children. For many years she desired a child with all her heart, so she went to Shiloh to pray at the Tabernacle. Hannah made this promise to God: "Lord, do not forget me. If You will give me a son, I will give him back to You, to serve You all his life."

Eli, the priest at the Tabernacle, saw Hannah's lips moving as she prayed. He thought she had taken too much wine. But when he learned of Hannah's prayers, he gave her his blessing. Hannah returned home with peace in her heart.

When did God call Samuel to be a prophet?

God heard Hannah's prayers and gave her a son. She named him Samuel. Keeping to her promise, she brought the boy to live with the priests.

Young Samuel slept outside Eli's room. One night, after Eli had gone to bed, a voice woke Samuel, calling his name. The boy ran to see what Eli needed. "I did not call you. Go back to bed," the priest said.

The voice called Samuel two more times, and Eli realized it was the Lord calling his young helper. Eli told Samuel to listen; God had a message for him. From that day on, God talked with Samuel. He became known throughout the land as a great prophet.

What is a prophet?

A prophet is a person called by God to deliver His message to the people. In the Old Testament, prophets told about the future, they served as leaders and advised the kings. Some prophets performed miracles and others wrote down God's words. Several books of the Bible were written by prophets: Jeremiah, Amos, Jonah, Micah and others. The prophets not only spoke God's words, they lived them out in their own lives.

The Old Testament is full of messages from prophets, but where are the prophets today? Some people think that there were prophets only in that time because that was the only way God could talk to His people. Today, we have God's written word, the Bible, and each of us can read His messages for ourselves.

Who were Phinehas and Hophni?

When God called the boy Samuel, he gave him a message about Phinehas and Hophni, Eli's sons. They were supposed to be priests of the Lord like their father. But Phinehas and Hophni did not love God. They laughed at His commands. Eli tried to correct his sons, but he could not control them.

In His message to Samuel, God said that Phinehas and Hophni would die by the sword together.

How did King Saul disobey God?

In his first years as the king of Israel, Saul was a very good leader. He was careful always to obey God's laws. Saul led his army to fight against soldiers from other countries, and God gave him victory after victory. But gradually, King Saul began to forget that his power came from the Lord.

Then Saul's army captured a town with many fine sheep and cattle. God commanded that everything, even these animals, be destroyed. Saul decided instead to send the sheep and cows home with his men. The prophet Samuel grew very angry. "Since you have turned away from God, He now turns away from you."

How did Samuel find the next king of Israel?

The Lord told Samuel to leave King Saul and travel to Bethlehem. There, God would show him the man to be the next king of Israel.

In Bethlehem, the prophet saw seven fine-looking young men. They were the sons of Jesse. One by one, Samuel looked at these handsome men and prayed to God. But the Lord answered, "Do not look at their faces, Samuel. God does not see the same way people see. The Lord looks at the heart."

Jesse had one more son who was out taking care of the sheep. When Samuel saw David, the Lord told him this young man would be the next king of Israel.

How did David become skilled with a slingshot?

As a shepherd, it was David's job to protect his sheep from attacks by wolves. He used a slingshot to do this. The slingshot was a patch of leather or cloth that had two braided cords on each end. The shepherd would place a smooth pebble in the patch and twirl the slingshot around his head. When he let go of one of the cords, the pebble would fly through the air like a deadly bullet.

David probably developed a strong arm and a good eye using his slingshot to kill the wild animals that attacked his flocks.

Why did Jesse send David to the battlefield?

When the Philistines again attacked Israel, Jesse's three oldest sons were old enough to fight in King Saul's army. Like any father, Jesse worried about them. Were they all right? Were they getting enough to eat? One day Jesse got word that the army was camped nearby. He packed some food and asked his youngest son, David, to deliver it to his brothers.

The shepherd boy traveled to the camp and learned that his brothers were out on the battlefield. He went to talk to them and saw for the first time the giant Philistine warrior Goliath.

How did David kill Goliath?

For forty days, the Philistine giant Goliath challenged the men of Israel: "I dare you feeble warriors! Send out a man to fight with me! I say that the one who loses will hand over his people to become slaves."

Goliath stood 9 feet, 4 inches tall. He wore a suit of armor that weighed 125 pounds, and carried two spears. Not one man among the Israelites would meet him in single combat. But when David arrived with food for his brothers, he could not understand the soldiers' fear. "Why does Goliath think he can speak against the army of the living God? He is no more dangerous than the wild animals which attack my father's sheep. I will fight him, and the Lord will surely be with me."

When King Saul saw that David was determined, he put his own armor on the boy and gave him his sword. But David was not used to these things. He went out to meet Goliath carrying only his own slingshot and five smooth stones he had picked up from a riverbed.

Goliath roared when he saw the shepherd boy. "Come, child! I will feed your body to the birds and the beasts!" The insults were still pouring from Goliath's mouth when the first stone smashed into his forehead. Goliath fell face down and David rushed up, seized the giant's sword and cut off his head.

How did David help King Saul sleep?

After David's defeat of Goliath, Saul took the young man to live with him at the palace. Saul grew to love him very much. During this time, the king was bothered with restless nights. It was because of Saul's disobedience that the spirit of the Lord had left him.

David was skilled at playing the harp. When Saul could not sleep, David would sit by his bed and play soft music. David became good friends with Saul's son Jonathan.

Why did Saul grow to hate David?

Saul and David fought many battles against the Philistines. David was very successful, and Saul put him in charge of the entire army. One day, a group of women greeted the soldiers as they returned home. The women sang, "Saul has killed his thousands, but David has killed tens of thousands!"

This song upset the king. As David's fame spread throughout the land, Saul began to hate him. He feared the people would make David their king. One night, when the young man came to play his harp, Saul hurled a spear across the room and tried to kill him.

David escaped that night and hid with the prophet Samuel, waiting for the day when he could lead the nation of Israel in righteousness.

How did Saul and Jonathan die?

Enemy soldiers attacked Israel and surrounded the king's army. Saul and his men fought bravely, but Jonathan and his brothers were killed. When Saul saw there was no hope for winning the battle, he fell upon his own sword and killed himself.

At this news, David remembered the good things about Saul. He remembered his love for Jonathan. He sang a song to honor them.

Oh, how mighty men have fallen!
We loved Saul and Jonathan.
They were faster than eagles, stronger than lions.
Oh, how the mighty have fallen.

Why did David dance in the streets of Jerusalem?

For seven years, David and his men fought against the other tribes of Israel. But at last, the people came together. "David, God has said you should rule the nation of Israel. We are ready for you to be our king."

The first thing David did was to capture the city of Jerusalem from the enemy. He built up the city and strengthened it. Next, David sent for the Ark of the Covenant. As soldiers brought the holy box containing the Ten Commandments into Jerusalem, people blew horns and sang for joy. King David himself danced in the streets.

What kindness did David show Jonathan's son?

When the fighting had stopped, King David asked, "Are there any people left in Saul's family? I want to be kind to them because of the great love I had for Jonathan."

David learned that Jonathan's son Mephibosheth still lived. He returned all of Saul's land to Mephibosheth and brought the young man to live at the palace.

"Do not fear me, Mephibosheth. I will show you kindness because your father was my best friend. There will always be food for you at my table."

Who was Bathsheba?

In all that David did, he brought honor to God until the evening he desired another man's wife. David was on his roof enjoying the breeze when he saw a beautiful woman bathing in her courtyard. His servants told him the woman was Bathsheba, the wife of a soldier in David's army. David could not get her out of his mind. At last, he sent for her, and she spent every night with the king while her husband was away at war. Bathsheba was carrying David's child. He started to worry. What would Bathsheba's husband do when he learned what had happened?

How did Bathsheba's husband die?

David decided to get rid of Uriah, Bathsheba's husband. Then he could have Bathesheba to himself. So the king ordered Uriah to go to the front of the battlelines, where the fighting was the fiercest. Uriah was a faithful soldier and he obeyed without questioning. He died in a battle, and almost no one knew that David had planned it that way.

King David thought his problems were over. He married Bathsheba and their son was born a few months later.

Who was Nathan?

Nathan was a prophet of the Lord. He was also David's friend. Nathan knew what David had done. He went to David, risking his own life to deliver God's message. "What I have to say will anger you," Nathan said. "I know you can order your men to kill me. But you have broken God's commandments. Now hear what trouble God will send to your house." And Nathan told David that Bathsheba's baby would die.

Why was David "a man after God's own heart?"

When David's and Bathsheba's baby died, David's heart overflowed with shame. He refused to eat and lay on the bare ground for seven nights, confessing to the Lord. God forgave him, and later David and Bathsheba had another son, Solomon.

David went on to rule Israel for many more years. He deeply loved the Lord and tried to serve Him in all that he did. That is why the Bible calls David "a man after God's own heart."

Who was Zadok?

When King David's sons grew up, they wanted their father's power and wealth for their own. They convinced other people to join them in rebellion. But through it all, a priest named Zadok remained loyal to David.

Zadok made sure the Ark of the Covenant traveled with David's army so God would be with them. David trusted Zadok and asked him to stay at the palace to keep an eye on his family. When at last David was ready to hand the country over to his son Solomon, it was Zadok who anointed Solomon king. For many generations, Zadok's descendants served the Lord as faithful priests.

Who built the Temple in Jerusalem?

When David enlarged the city of Jerusalem, he wanted to build a permanent place of worship for the Lord, but God did not allow him to do this. Instead, God said, David's job was to collect the fine woods, gold and gems needed for the Temple. Then David's son Solomon would direct the building when he became king.

Solomon's men labored for seven years to build an earthly Temple that would show some of the glory of God's heavenly Temple. People from far and wide came to marvel at this wondrous house of prayer in Jerusalem.

Why was Solomon known as the wisest man on earth?

Solomon followed in the ways of his father, King David. He worshipped the Lord and honored Him with many sacrifices. One night the Lord spoke to Solomon in a dream. "Ask for anything you want, Solomon. I will give it to you."

Solomon's reply pleased the Lord: "My God, I am like a child. I do not know enough to be a good leader. So I ask You to give me wisdom. Then I will know what is right for Your people."

God gave Solomon the wisdom he requested. People from many nations came to listen to his wise words. And the Lord blessed the king with riches and honor as well.

Why did Solomon threaten to cut a baby in half?

Two women brought a baby to Solomon. They both claimed to be the baby's mother and they argued back and forth. Solomon listened to them for a few minutes, then asked for a sword. "There is only one way to be fair. Cut the baby in half and give each woman a piece of the child!"

"No, no!" one of the women screamed. "Do not kill the child! Give the baby to her, but just do not hurt him!"

Every one at the king's court that day knew that woman was the real mother.

Why did the Queen of Sheba visit Solomon?

Word of King Solomon's great wisdom spread throughout the world, even as far away as Africa. The rich and powerful Queen of Sheba decided she would test Solomon's wisdom for herself. She loaded her camels with costly gifts and traveled over 1,000 miles to Israel.

When she entered Jerusalem and saw the palace and the great Temple, she was amazed. The stories she had heard about Solomon's wealth were true! Solomon graciously received the African queen. They talked of many things. "Your wisdom is even greater than your wealth!" the queen exclaimed. "The God of Israel is indeed a powerful God!"

Why did the nation of Israel split into two kingdoms?

King David had united the tribes of Israel into one powerful nation. Solomon ruled wisely and kept the nation together. But when Solomon died, his son Rehoboam gave harsh commands, and some of the people chose their own leader. The divided kingdoms were known as Israel, to the north, and Judah, to the south. Sometimes the two kingdoms fought each other and other times they lived in peace. But after a time, armies from enemy countries defeated both kingdoms and carried the best of the people away. The Israelites never came together as one independent nation again until this century.

Who was Jezebel?

Jezebel was the wife of King Ahab, ruler of the Northern Kingdom. She was from the land of Sidon and worshipped the false god Baal by sacrificing young children. When she began building altars to her god in Israel, the prophet Elijah spoke out against her. She planned many ways to kill him. Jezebel also stirred her husband and son to do terrible things. After they were killed by their enemies, she dressed herself up and tried to make the new king marry her. Even to this day, her name is used to describe a thoroughly wicked woman.

How did ravens take care of Elijah?

Ahab and his wife Jezebel did more things to anger God than any of the rulers before them. Elijah went to Ahab and delivered God's message: no rain or dew would fall on the land for three years. Then God told Elijah to leave the king and go live alone by the brook of Cherith. There, ravens brought the prophet his food morning and night, and Elijah drank from the brook. While Ahab and the rest of the country went without water, God cared for His faithful messenger.

What book made King Josiah cry?

Many years passed, and the people of Judah turned once again to worship false gods. There was no one left who remembered how to honor the Lord. Then a young boy named Josiah became king. God spoke to his heart. When he was 18, Josiah ordered men to clean out the Temple, which had not been used for many years. The workers found an old dusty scroll, the book of the Law of Moses. King Josiah cried when he heard the words from the book, for he saw how far his people had strayed from the Lord.

What did Huldah promise King Josiah?

After Josiah had heard the words from the book of the Law, he sent a message to the prophetess Huldah. He wanted to know if the words were true.

Huldah sent this answer: "Josiah, the words in that scroll are indeed the teachings of the Lord. He is angry at the people for worshipping idols and He will destroy them. But because of your tears, the Lord will hold back His anger. He will not destroy Judah while you are king."

Then Josiah gathered all the people together, young and old, great and small.

He read to them all the words from the book of the Law. Then all the people promised to obey the Lord's commands.

Who destroyed the Temple and burned Jerusalem?

After many years of leading the people to honor God, Josiah died and two of his sons ruled Judah. Then King Nebuchadnezzar of Babylon attacked Jerusalem, just as the Lord had promised. His army surrounded the walls and allowed no food into the city. For four months, the people starved. When they were too weak to fight, the Babylonian army stormed into the city and removed all the treasures from the Temple. They led away the leaders and the skilled workers. Then the soldiers set fire to the buildings. Everything of importance burned to the ground.

Where were the Hebrew people taken when Jerusalem was destroyed?

When the Babylonian army returned home, they took with them many of the Israelites. They chose people with skills or education, who could enrich the nation of Babylon. The transplanted Jews started out as servants, but many of them worked and became prosperous businessmen or trusted court officials. Still, Babylon was not home, and the Israelites always longed to return to the land God had given their fathers.

The people left behind in Jerusalem struggled just to stay alive. They had no leaders left, and no place where they could worship the Lord.

Who rebuilt the foundation of the Temple?

When the Israelites journeyed back to their homeland in 539 B. C., they found Jerusalem in ruins. Their first job was to set up an altar and offer sacrifices to the Lord. Then the people scattered to build homes and plant crops. A year later, Zerubbabel, a grandson of the king, and the priest Jeshua gathered the people to work on the foundation for a new Temple. When the stones were in place, the priests blew their trumpets as in days long past. Young people shouted for joy, but the older ones cried, remembering the great Temple that was no more.

How did Ezra lead his people back to God?

Fifty years passed, and progress in Jerusalem was slow. The Temple had been rebuilt, but the people were not faithful to the Lord. Many of the men had married pagan women and worshipped their gods. Ezra was a Jew of high position in the Babylonian court. He learned of the great needs among his people who had returned to their homeland years before.

Ezra gathered the Jews still living in Babylon and led a second group back. He cleaned the Temple, teaching the priests how to make proper offerings to the Lord. He read from the law of Moses. Because of his earnest prayer and preaching, the people in Jerusalem returned to the faith of their fathers.

Who plotted to destroy the Jews of Babylon?

Even though many Jews returned to Israel, some remained in Babylon because of their good jobs and important positions. But they always tried to keep the ways of their fathers and honor the Lord.

When Xerxes ruled Babylon, he appointed a man named Haman to serve as his chancellor. Haman enjoyed the power of his job and ordered all the people of the land to bow before him. The Jews believed it was right only to bow to the Lord, so they refused to obey. Haman was furious and issued orders that all the Jews be put to death.

Why did Xerxes put aside his queen?

While Haman was plotting to kill the Jews, King Xerxes had troubles of his own. His wife did not want to be with him, so he sent her away. For a long time, Xerxes hated women because of the trouble with his wife. But at last he grew lonely and wished for someone to love.

The king's servants brought to the court the most beautiful ladies in all the land. One of them was Esther, a young Jewish woman. Xerxes chose Esther to be his wife and he loved her very much, but he did not realize she was a Jew.

How did Queen Esther save her people?

Mordecai was Esther's uncle. He had taken care of her from the time she was a little girl. When Esther became queen, Mordecai saw a way to save the Jews. He sent a message to his niece, telling her of Haman's order to kill those who would not bow before him.

This news saddened Esther, but there was nothing she could do. In those days, a queen did not get involved in matters of law. To tell Xerxes about the problem might make him very angry. But Mordecai sent Esther a second message: "Do not think you can escape this problem, niece. Someday Xerxes will discover that you are a Jew, and he kill you because you do not bow before men. Perhaps God has made you queen just so you could help our people."

Esther went without food for three days and prayed to the Lord. Finally, she put on her most beautiful robes and stood outside the king's door. When Xerxes saw her, he asked what she wanted. Esther invited him to a banquet and when the king had feasted for two days, she told him about the evil order that Haman had issued. Esther explained that she too would die because she was a Jew and would bow only before the Lord. Then Xerxes ordered that the law be changed. Haman was hanged and his job was given to Mordecai, Esther's uncle. The queen herself declared a day of celebration for all the Jews in Babylon.

When was Jeremiah called to be a prophet?

Jeremiah lived during the last days of the nation of Judah. When he was 21 years old, he learned about God's plan for his life. God told Jeremiah he had been chosen to be a prophet since before his birth. He was to speak the word of the Lord to kings and nations.

At first, Jeremiah did not want this job. He wanted to live a simple happy life. But he felt the Lord's hand upon him, so he took the message of God's judgment to the people. Jeremiah never married or enjoyed a comfortable home. When Jerusalem was destroyed by the Babylonians, Jeremiah fled to Egypt. Even in his last days, the prophet faithfully declared the word of the Lord.

Why did Jehoiakim cut Jeremiah's scroll in pieces?

Jeremiah spoke the Lord's words to the people of Judah, but they did not listen. So God told the prophet to send a scroll to King Jehoiakim. Jeremiah's friend, Baruch, worked many hours writing down the messages that God had given Jeremiah. Perhaps now the king would pay attention!

An officer of the court took the scroll and began reading it out loud before Jehoiakim. As he listened, the disobedient king cut each message off the scroll. One by one, God's words to his people landed in the fire.

Jeremiah and Baruch prepared another scroll so that people who came after them would know of the Lord's warnings to the nation of Judah.

Which Old Testament book mourns the destruction of Jerusalem?

Lamentations is a collection of sad songs written after the Babylonian army had burned the city of Jerusalem. In these songs, the poet sorrowfully explains that the destruction was God's punishment for sin. But the book of Lamentations is also hopeful, because it tells about God's great faithfulness to His people. His mercy on us begins new every morning; His compassion and care never fail.

Which prophet was given a scroll to eat?

When the Babylonians captured Jerusalem, they took many of the Israelites to work as their servants. One of them was a young man named Ezekiel. As he worked digging a canal beside the Chebar River, the sky opened and Ezekiel saw visions of the glory of God. The Lord held out a scroll, "Son of man, eat this scroll. Go speak unto the house of Israel."

Ezekiel obeyed and ate the book. It tasted as sweet as honey in his mouth. Then with a rustle of great wings and the turning of heavenly chariot wheels, the Lord departed, leaving Ezekiel in a state of shock. For a week, the young man thought of nothing but what he had seen. But then he knew he had to share this vision with his people. For the rest of his life, the prophet preached to the Jews in Babylon about the Lord's greatness and His promise to return them to Israel.

Who was Daniel?

Like Ezekiel, Daniel was one of the Jews who was taken to Babylon when Jerusalem was attacked. While Ezekiel worked at hard physical labor, Daniel lived out his life in the palace, advising the Babylonian leaders. He started out as a prisoner, but ended up second only to the king. Even in a pagan palace, Daniel remained true to the Lord.

Why did Daniel refuse to eat the king's food?

When the Jews arrived in Babylon, King Nebuchadnezzar's servant picked young men to live at the palace. Only the strongest and most intelligent were chosen. These youths trained with experts so one day they could become officers of the court. Daniel and three friends were selected. At the palace, they were served rich food from the king's own table.

But Daniel knew this food had probably been blessed in the temple of a false god. Eating it would not honor the Lord. So Daniel asked for vegetables and water. The servant finally agreed to let Daniel and his friends eat simple meals for ten days. At the end of that time, King Nebuchadnezzar tested all the young men. He found that none were as healthy and strong as Daniel and his friends.

How did Daniel learn the secret of Nebuchadnezzar's first dream?

Shortly after Daniel came to live at the palace, Nebuchadnezzar was troubled by a dream. The king awoke knowing he had dreamed something very important, but he could not remember what it was. He summoned all the wise men in Babylon. No one could tell the king what he had dreamed.

Then Daniel heard of the problem. He went to his friends and asked them to pray that God would reveal the king's dream to him. That night, in answer to their prayers, the Lord explained the secret to Daniel in a vision.

How did Daniel's friends escape death by fire?

King Nebuchadnezzar built an enormous figure of gold. He ordered the people to worship the statue. Daniel's friends, Shadrach, Meshach and Abednego, did not obey this command. So Nebuchadnezzar had the three men tied up and thrown into a blazing furnace.

Later on, the king looked into the furnace, expecting to see nothing left but blackened bones. Instead, Nebuchadnezzar saw the men walking around, their faces not the least bit burnt. And someone was with them, an angel sent by God to protect them from the flames.

When the king released the three men from the furnace, he cried, "These men trusted in their God and He saved them! For now on, no one shall be allowed to speak against the God of Shadrach, Meshach and Abednego!"

Why did Darius put Daniel in the lions' den?

Daniel served three kings of Babylon: Nebuchadnezzar, Belshazzar and Darius. Darius trusted the prophet and put him in charge of 120 officers of the court. These men did not like having a Jew over them, so they plotted to get rid of Daniel. They went to the king with a new law they had written. It said that people could not pray unless they prayed to the king. Darius made this the law throughout the land.

When Daniel heard about the new law, he continued to pray to God three times a day as he had always done. The officers took him before the king. Darius loved Daniel, but he had no choice except to obey his own law. He had the prophet thrown into a den of hungry lions.

Early the next morning, the king rushed to the lions' den. When he found that God had saved Daniel from the lions, he wrote a letter to all his people. "Daniel's God is the living God. He rescues people and does miracles. Respect and honor the God of Daniel."

Who was Jonah?

Of all the prophets, Jonah was the most stubborn. Many of the men God called did not think they were good enough to do His work, but Jonah actually tried to run away from the Lord!

Jonah lived in the Northern Kingdom during the time of Elisha. He helped King Jereboam get back territory that had been lost in battle. One day, God told him to go and preach in Nineveh, the capital of Assyria. As a Jew, Jonah hated the Assyrians. He did not want to tell the enemy about the Lord!

Instead, Jonah decided to head in the opposite direction. He went to Joppa and found a ship that was going to Tarshish.

How did God punish Jonah for running away?

As soon as Jonah got on board the ship, a terrible storm arose. When the sailors learned that Jonah was running from his God, they threw him overboard. But God did not allow Jonah to drown. Instead, a huge fish swallowed him. Jonah stayed inside the fish for three days and three nights.

At last the prophet was ready to do God's work, so the Lord spoke to the fish. It spit Jonah out on dry land.

Which book bridges the Old and New Testaments?

Malachi is the last prophet of the Old Testament. He lived 100 years after the people returned to Israel from captivity in Babylon. After the difficult days of rebuilding their land, the people slipped into carelessness again. They did not honor their own husbands and wives. They cheated workers of their pay and robbed from poor widows and orphans. They did not think God saw these things.

But Malachi reminded the Jews of the Lord's great love and blessing. "Behold, I will send My messenger, and he shall prepare the way before Me: and the Lord will come to His Temple. On that day, the proud and the evil will be burned like straw. And He shall turn the heart of the fathers back to the children, and the heart of the children to their fathers."

How many years passed between the Old and the New Testaments?

Four hundred years stretched between Old and New Testament times. During all this period, the nation of Israel was not its own. Stronger armies took over the land. The Jewish people suffered greatly under foreign rulers. They were forbidden to worship in the Temple and forced to eat unclean food.

People remembered the promises of their prophets. Someday God would send the Messiah to set them free. "How long, O Lord?" they cried.

What is the Gospel?

The meaning of the word "Gospel" is good news, and it refers to the good news that Jesus came from God to be the Savior of a world dying from its sin. The first four books of the New Testament, Matthew, Mark, Luke and John, are called the Gospels because they tell about the life, death and resurrection of Jesus Christ.

Who wrote the four Gospels?

The Gospels are named after the men who were thought to have writtten them. Matthew, the author of the first Gospel, was a tax collector. He was well-educated and probably very wealthy. He gave up everything to follow Jesus.

The second Gospel was written by Mark. He and his mother were among the first people to believe in Jesus. Later, Mark traveled with Barnabas and Paul, spreading the news that God had sent His son to die for the sins of the world.

Luke was a doctor. He also traveled with Paul. He wrote the book of Acts as well as the third Gospel.

The author of the fourth Gospel was another disciple, John. He and his brother James had followed John the Baptist until they met Jesus. He did not write his Gospel until he was an old man living on a barren island.

How are the four Gospels different from each other?

Each of the four Gospel writers told the story of Jesus, but each man told it in his own way. By reading all four Gospels, we can get a more complete picture of what God's Son was like when He lived on earth.

Matthew had Jewish readers in mind when he wrote his book. He showed that Jesus was the Messiah King because He fulfilled Old Testament prophecies. Mark thought about people who had power, like the Roman rulers in Israel. He wrote that the most powerful One of all, Jesus, came to help people. Mark emphasized Jesus' actions. Luke wanted his Greek friends to know that Jesus was God and man. He gave many details about Jesus' life. John's Gospel is a little different from the other three because he wrote mainly about Jesus' thoughts and prayers. John wrote to people everywhere, to help them understand the ideas that Jesus taught.

Why does the New Testament list the ancestors of Jesus?

Both Matthew and Luke list the family members who came before Jesus. Matthew shows that Jesus was related to Abraham, King David, Ruth and others. Luke traces Jesus' ancestors all the way back to Adam, the first man. Jesus Christ came from a family filled with a variety of people, some good and some not so good. The Gospel writers wanted to show that God used all kinds of people to bring His Son into the world.

How did Mary learn of God's plan for her life?

God sent the angel Gabriel to Mary, a young woman who lived with her parents in Nazareth, a small town in Galilee. Mary was frightened when she first saw the angel, but Gabriel said, "Fear not, Mary, for God is pleased with you. You will have a son and His name shall be Jesus. He will rule over the people of Jacob forever."

"How can I have a baby?" Mary asked, "I am not married."

And Gabriel answered, "With God, nothing is impossible. The Holy Spirit will come upon you and cause the baby to be born. He will be a holy child, the Son of God."

Mary bowed before Gabriel. "I will serve the Lord. Let this happen as you have said."

Why did Joseph think about leaving Mary?

Joesph and Mary were engaged to be married. When Joseph learned that Mary was pregnant, he became very sad. How could Mary do this to him? To have another man's baby while she was engaged to Joseph was not right. Joseph quietly decided to call off their engagement.

But as Joseph was thinking this, an angel came to him in a dream. "Do not be afraid to marry Mary," the angel said. "She is a good woman. The baby is from the Holy Spirit. When He is born, you must name Him Jesus, for He will save people from their sins."

Why did Mary and Joseph travel to Bethlehem?

At this time, all the people of Israel were ordered to register with the tax collectors. Each family had to go to its hometown to sign up. Joseph was from the family of King David, who had been born in Bethlehem, so Mary and Joseph traveled there.

It was there that Jesus was born, just as the prophet Micah had foretold:

> But thou, Bethlehem, though thou be little among the thousands of Judah, yet out of thee shall come forth He that is to be ruler in Israel.

Who ruled Israel during New Testament days?

Rome conquered the nation of Israel in 63 B. C. Caesar, the Roman emperor, made the little country part of his huge empire that stretched from Egypt to what is now Italy and France. Roman soldiers were sent to every country to make sure that Caesar's laws were carried out and that taxes were collected.

Caesar ordered that the people in his empire treat him like a god. The Israelites refused to worship anyone but God, and so suffered under the Roman's laws.

To help him rule this rebellious country, Caesar appointed a ruler named Herod. King Herod was from Edom, the region just south of Israel, and he knew all the customs and religious laws of the Jews. He could have helped make things better, but Herod cared only for keeping his throne and pleasing Caesar.

And she brought forth her firstborn son, and wrapped him in swaddling clothes, and laid him in a manger; because there was no room for them in the inn.

Luke 2:7

What are swaddling clothes?

As soon as Jesus was born, Mary wrapped Him tightly in swaddling clothes. These were long strips of cloth that mothers wound around their babies. Being wrapped this way kept the babies warm. It also made them feel cozy and protected. Swaddling clothes served as diapers and blankets all in one.

Mothers would just wrap their babies in clean strips whenever they needed changing.

What is a manger?

A manger is a feeding box for cattle, sheep, donkeys, or horses. Most mangers in Bible times were cut from rock or made out of stones cemented together. Families often built their houses on two levels and placed a manger on the lower level for their animals. Other times, they would use a cave for a barn, and put a manger inside.

Because the little village of Bethlehem was overflowing with people registering for taxes, Mary and Joseph had to stay in a stable, probably just a cave with a manger.

Who were the Wise Men?

The Gospel of Matthew tells the story of the Wise Men, the Magi. They were most likely scholars from Persia who learned of the birth of a new king by studying the stars. They traveled first to Jerusalem, seeking the newborn king at Herod's palace. There they learned about the Old Testament prophecy that a king would be born in Bethlehem. So they traveled on to the small village and presented gifts of frankincense and myrrh to the baby sleeping in the stable. The Bible does not say how many Wise Men came to see Jesus, but many people believe there were three.

What is frankincense?

Frankincense is an expensive perfume made from the sap of the balsam tree. It was used in worship at the Temple to offer a pleasing fragrance to God. This costly perfume, brought by the Wise Men, showed that baby Jesus was worthy of their worship.

What is myrrh?

Myrrh is a thick, sweet-smelling liquid that comes from an African tree. In Bible days, its main use was in preparing a dead body for burial. Myrrh was rubbed on the skin. Then the body was wrapped in cloth and placed in a grave.

One of the Wise Men brought myrrh to the stable. This gift pointed to Jesus' death on the cross.

Who saw baby Jesus at the Temple?

When Jesus was a little more than a month old, Mary and Joseph took Him to the Temple to present Him to the Lord. All good Jewish parents did this for their new baby boys. Two elderly people, Simeon and Anna, were worshipping there when Jesus' family arrived.

Simeon had long prayed for the time when God would help Israel. He took the baby in his arms. "Thank you, Lord! Now I can die in peace, for I have seen Your salvation with my own eyes."

Anna was a prophetess who prayed to God day and night. She told everyone that she had seen the child who would free Jerusalem.

Hearing these words, Mary and Joseph were filled with wonder.

Why did King Herod fear baby Jesus?

Herod had lived in Palestine all his life. He had heard the messages of the prophets. He knew that the Jews were waiting for a Messiah to come, the person who would bring peace to Israel. When the Wise Men stopped at the palace to ask about a newborn king, they stirred up Herod's fear and jealousy. Would this child grow up to take Herod's throne away from him?

Herod made a great show of pointing the three kings to Bethlehem, but he also asked them to report back when they found the child. He had a plan.

How did Mary and Joseph save Jesus from Herod?

When the Wise Men did not return to tell Herod about the baby they found, the king took action. Determined that no child would become king in his place, Herod ordered that all baby boys in Bethlehem be killed. At this same time, however, an angel appeared to Joseph in a dream and told him to go to the land of Egypt. Joseph and Mary packed their belongings and made the long journey with the new baby. There were many Jews living in Egypt at that time; Joseph may have settled his family with them.

Back in Bethlehem, the cries of mothers weeping over small bodies filled the air.

Where did Jesus' family settle when they returned from Egypt?

Several years passed and King Herod died. An angel of the Lord appeared to Joseph in a dream and told him it was safe to return to Israel. So the family packed up again. As they neared their homeland, Joseph heard that one of Herod's evil sons, Archelaus, ruled Judea. They decided not to return to Bethlehem. Instead they traveled further north, back to Mary's village of Nazareth in Galilee. There they made their home.

What trade did Jesus learn?

As Jesus grew, He worked in Joseph's carpentry shop. He learned to use tools such as a saw, a hammer and an adze, a cutting tool similar to an axe. In Bible times, a carpenter's chief work was making furniture, doors, fence posts and handles for farm tools.

Who was John the Baptist?

John the Baptist was Jesus' cousin, the son of Elizabeth and Zechariah. Before the time he was born, his parents knew he had been chosen by God for a special job. When he grew up, John went to live by himself in the wilderness, to listen for God's words. All he had to eat were the foods he could gather, locust pods and wild honey. He made his own clothing from camel's hair, as the prophet Elijah of old had done. It was not an easy life, but the Lord gave John an important message. The young man began preaching, and many people went out to the desert to hear him.

"Repent!" John told them. "Change your hearts and lives, for the kingdom of heaven is coming soon! Turn away from the wrong things you do and be baptized. Let God cleanse you of your sins."

Many who heard asked God to forgive their sin. They wanted John to baptize them to show that their hearts had been changed.

What special job did John the Baptist do?

When people heard John the Baptist preach, many thought he was the Messiah who would save Israel. But John told them he was only a messenger who announced the coming of someone much greater. "My job is to baptize you with water," John said. "But God is sending someone who will baptize with the Holy Spirit. He will save those people who are like good grain, but he will destroy those who are trash in the grain."

One day, Jesus came out to the wilderness to be baptized. John stared into His face. "Lord, why do You come to me? I should be baptized by You!"

But Jesus answered, "Let us do this, John, to be right in all things."

So John baptized Jesus in the Jordan River.

How did God show His pleasure at Jesus' baptism?

In being baptized, Jesus showed that He was ready to do His Father's work. As He came up out of the water, the sky above opened. Jesus saw the Holy Spirit coming down in the form of a dove.

The dove rested on Jesus' head, and a voice from heaven said, "This is My Son and I love Him. I am well pleased with Him today."

How did Jesus choose His disciples?

Jesus began to travel through the countryside, talking about God, His Father. Everywhere He went, crowds gathered and people asked many questions. Jesus knew He needed help, so He went up on a mountain alone to pray. All night, He prayed about choosing the right men to help Him teach and preach and heal in His Father's name.

The next morning, Jesus came down from the mountain and chose twelve men from those who had followed Him: Peter, James, John, Andrew, Philip, Bartholomew, Matthew, Thomas, a second James, Thaddeus, Simon, and Judas.

Which disciples were fishermen?

Four of the disciples worked as fishermen: Peter, Andrew, James, and John. The men had just brought their boats to shore when Jesus came to them. "Go back out," Jesus said. "And you will catch fish."

Peter answered, "Sir, we worked hard fishing all night and did not catch a single thing. But we will do as you say." The men sailed back out onto the Sea of Galilee and let down their nets. They caught so many fish, the nets began to break. The fishermen looked at Jesus with amazement and fear.

"Do not be afraid," Jesus said. "Follow me, and I will make you fishers of men."

What was Jesus' first miracle?

Soon after Jesus had picked His disciples, He went to a wedding in the nearby village of Cana. Friends were there to help the young couple celebrate, and there was much feasting and dancing. During the party, Mary, Jesus' mother, saw that all the wine was gone. She told Jesus.

"It is not yet my time," He said. But Mary whispered to the servants to do whatever Jesus said.

Jesus asked the servants to fill six large jars with water. They served some of that water to the man in charge of the party. "This is splendid wine!" the man cried. "Why have you saved it so long?"

Only a few people at the wedding knew what had happened. But Jesus' disciples saw, and they began to believe in Him.

Did Jesus' neighbors accept Him as the Son of God?

When Jesus taught about the Scriptures, many people were amazed. The words seemed to make sense to them for the first time. It was as if He really knew God! But that was impossible - Jesus was just the son of Joseph the carpenter.

Jesus scolded the people. "A prophet is not accepted in his own town. You do not believe in Me just as people long ago did not believe in the prophets Elijah and Elisha." This angered Jesus' neighbors, and they chased Him away.

Why was the Temple a den of thieves?

Soon it was time for Passover. Jesus went with His disciples to Jerusalem, to worship at the great Temple. There in the courtyard, people bought birds, sheep and oxen to offer as sacrifices, and money-changers traded local coins with people from other places.

When Jesus saw all this buying and selling in His Father's house, He grew angry. The Temple was supposed to be a house of prayer, not a marketplace! Jesus knocked over the tables and sent the merchants running from the courtyard. "Away, you crooks!" He shouted. "You have turned the Temple into a hideout for robbers!"

Why did Jesus speak of rebuilding the Temple?

When Jesus chased the merchants from the Temple court, a curious crowd gathered. They asked Jesus for a sign, to prove He had the right to do this. Jesus quietly said, "If this Temple were destroyed, I could rebuild it in three days' time."

The people gasped. "Impossible! It took 46 years to build the Temple!"

Then Jesus left the courtyard and went throughout the city of Jerusalem, healing and teaching. From that day on, the crowd followed Him everywhere He went. Later, when He rose from the dead in three days' time, they remembered His words. The Temple Jesus had been speaking about was His very own body.

Who were the Pharisees?

In New Testament days, the Pharisees were people who believed in following the religious laws as completely as they could. Since the time of Moses, hundreds of rules had been added, so being a Pharisee was hard work.

Because the Pharisees studied the Scripture so much, they considered themselves better than most people. But Jesus said, "Do not be like the Pharisees. Their lives look good on the outside, but inside they are like boxes of bones and dirty things. You should not try to feel more important than another person. You are all brothers and sisters, with one heavenly Father."

Which Pharisee secretly came to see Jesus?

Nicodemus was one of the Pharisee leaders in Jerusalem. Passing through a crowd one day, he heard Jesus speak about the new life God wants for each of us. This idea troubled Nicodemus. He waited until night would hide where he was going and went to see Jesus.

"I am an old man. Many years have passed since I was born to my mother. Tell me, Rabbi, how can I get a new life?"

Jesus answered, "Nicodemus, there is more to life than skin and bones. You also have a spirit. It must be brought to life by the water of baptism and by the Holy Spirit. If a person does not have two births – body and spirit – he cannot enter God's kingdom."

How did Jesus calm the storm?

People crowded around Jesus everywhere He went. To have time with the disciples, He sometimes sailed out on the Sea of Galilee. One evening, after Jesus had fallen asleep in the boat, a furious storm arose. Several of the disciples had lived by the sea all their lives; they knew how to handle a boat in rough weather. But the storm was so bad, even these men were scared. They woke Jesus.

He looked at their frightened faces. "You men of little faith, why are you so afraid?" Then He spoke to the sea.

The storm immediately stopped. "What kind of man is this?" the disciples said. "Even the winds and the waves obey Him!"

Who walked on water with Jesus?

Another time, the disciples were in a boat by themselves when fierce winds began to blow. Standing on shore, Jesus saw that they were in trouble. He walked across the sea and stood by the boat. The men were terrified. They thought they were seeing a ghost, not Jesus. Peter said, "Lord, if that is really You, let me walk out beside You. "

Peter stepped out of the boat and began to walk on the waves. But the minute he took his eyes off Jesus and looked at the rough water, he began to sink. Jesus caught him.

"Truly, You are the Son of God!" Peter cried.

Who are the Gentiles?

The Bible divides people into two groups: the Jews and the Gentiles. The Gentiles are all the people of the world who are not Jewish.

In the Old Testament, God revealed Himself to the Jews. He called them His chosen ones and used them to show all people the right way to live. So that the Jews would not leave God's ways, leaders like Moses and Joshua ordered that the people live apart from the Gentiles.

By New Testament days, religious law forbid a Jewish teacher from even speaking to a Gentile. But Jesus taught that God loved all people, Jew and Gentile alike.

How was a soldier's servant healed?

It was in Capernaum that Jesus healed the servant of a Roman officer. The commander respectfully approached Jesus and told Him about his servant who was ill. Jesus said He would go to the officer's home.

The Roman commander shook his head. "That is not necessary, Lord. It is not right, according to your law, that You enter the house of a Gentile. I understand power. I rule over many soldiers. When I give an order, it is done. All you need to do, Lord, is give the command and I know my servant will be healed."

Jesus was amazed at this man's words. "Truly, I have not found faith like this among my own people! Go home. Your servant has been healed."

Why did parents bring their children to Jesus?

When Jesus explained the Scriptures, people understood them in a new way. Parents wanted their children to hear Jesus, and they brought their families to receive His blessing. The disciples tried to turn the children away. "He is much too busy with important matters," they said.

"Let the children come to Me!" Jesus cried. He gently lifted a small girl in His arms and turned to the grown-ups. "Unless you come to your Heavenly Father with the simple heart of a child, you will never get into His Kingdom."

Jesus gathered the other children on to His lap. "Each of these little ones is very important to God. Anyone who helps a child in My Name helps Me."

What is a parable?

A parable is a story about earthly things that teaches a lesson about heavenly things.

Jesus often used parables because the stories caught people's attention. Even folks who were not religious could listen to a parable and learn from it. Sometimes, the meaning of a parable puzzled people, and they had to think about the story for a long time. The Good Samaritan, The Prodigal Son, The Good Soil and The House Built on the Rock are some of the parables Jesus told.

Who was the Good Samaritan?

Jesus told a parable about a kind man from Samaria, a man most Jews would consider an enemy. The story went like this:

Once upon a time a Jew was traveling on a lonely road when he was attacked by robbers. They took everything he had, beat him, and left him beside the road to die. Soon a priest from the Temple came down this very same road. He saw the man lying in a pool of blood, but the priest did not stop. A short time later, a Temple helper passed by. He also saw the man and heard his groans. But the Temple helper did not stop either.

Finally, a Samaritan came down the road on his donkey. When he saw the injured Jew, he washed the man's wounds and helped him up on the donkey. The Samaritan led the man to an inn and cared for him there that night. The next morning, the Samaritan left money with the innkeeper to pay for any medicine or food that the man might need.

Jesus asked His listeners, "Which of these men was a good neighbor?"

"The Samaritan," they answered.

"Then go and do the same thing he did!" Jesus said.

Who was the Prodigal Son?

In a story that Jesus told, the Prodigal Son was a rich young man who left home and spent his inheritance on fine clothes and parties. His money soon ran out, and the young man grew so hungry, he went to work for a farmer. He would have gladly eaten the scraps thrown to the pigs, but no one gave him anything. Finally the young man came to his senses and returned home. "Father," he said, "I have done wrong, and wasted all my inheritance. Just let me be one of your servants."

But the father greeted his son with arms open wide. "Bring fine clothes! Prepare a great feast! I feared my son was dead, but he is alive!"

How did the older son feel about his brother?

The older son was out in the fields when he heard music and laughter. He learned that his younger brother had come home and the family was celebrating. "Father, this is not fair!" he cried. "I have worked hard all the time my brother was out wasting your money. But you have never given a feast to honor me!"

The father replied, "Dear son, all that I have is yours. But it is right this day to be glad, for your brother who was lost is now found."

Jesus told this parable to show how God feels when one sinner turns back to the Lord.

Who climbed a tree so he could see Jesus?

Zacchaeus was a wealthy tax collector who lived in the city of Jericho. When he heard that Jesus was passing through the city, Zacchaeus joined the crowd waiting beside the road. But the tax collector was a short man; he knew he would not be able to see over the heads of the others waiting for Jesus. So Zacchaeus ran ahead and climbed a tree further down the road. When Jesus passed by, He stopped under the very tree where Zacchaeus waited.

Jesus looked up. "Come down, Zacchaeus! I would like to spend the evening at your house."

Zacchaeus was so excited, he quickly scrambled down the tree. He took Jesus home and offered Him the finest foods and the best bed in the house. Jesus spent the evening talking with the tax collector, and the next morning, Zacchaeus announced, "I have done wrong. I have grown rich collecting too much tax money. I will give half of what I have to the poor. Those I have cheated, I will pay back four times over!"

The good people of Jericho could not understand why Jesus would nd time with a dishonest person like Zacchaeus, but Jesus said, "I cam lost people and save them."

Why did Jesus heal a man on the Sabbath?

One of the Jews' most important laws came from the book of Genesis: to honor the Sabbath and keep it holy. By Jesus' day, the priests had added to this law a list of many things people could not do on the Sabbath. When Jesus saw a man with a deformed hand worshipping in the synagogue, He went over to heal him. Someone asked, "Is it right to work at healing on the Sabbath?"

Jesus answered him, "If your sheep falls into a ditch on the Sabbath, it is lawful for you to work and get it out. Surely a man is more important than sheep! It is lawful to honor God by doing good things any time we can — even on the Sabbath."

Who was Mary Magdalene?

When Jesus first met Mary Magdalene, she suffered from mental illness. After Jesus healed her, Mary became one of His most faithful followers. She spent her own money to buy food for Jesus and the disciples.

When Jesus was put to death on the cross, most of His followers ran away. But Mary Magdalene stayed. She com ed Jesus' mother, and helped M His body in the tomb. Mary son ene was the very first per the de Jesus after He rose from

What did Jesus send the disciples out to do?

After the disciples had been with Jesus for a time, He called them together. "I give you My power," He said. "Go to the people of Israel. Be good shepherds to them, for they are like lost sheep. Heal the sick. Give dead people life again. And tell people that the kingdom of heaven is coming soon!"

The disciples were excited and eager to help Jesus. "In the days ahead," He warned them, "You will be beaten because of Me. You will be arrested and taken before judges. People will hate you. But don't be afraid. Anyone who gives up his life for Me will have life everlasting in heaven!"

How did John the Baptist die?

John the Baptist had been chosen by God to announce the coming of His Son.

He also preached about the evil deeds of King Herod and his wife, Herodias. Herod threw the prophet in prison, but even stone walls could not silence John. Queen Heriodias finally had an idea. At a party for her husband, she told her daughter Salome to dance. This pleased the king and he offered Salome a reward. "Bring me the head of John the Baptist on a plate!" she cried.

Herod feared killing a man of God, but he granted Salome's request.

How did Jesus feed huge crowds of people?

The New Testament tells of two different times when Jesus fed the people who came to hear Him preach.

The news of John the Baptist's death made Jesus very sad. He took a boat across the Sea of Galilee to a quiet lonely place. Even then, thousands of people crowded around to hear His healing words. It grew late, and the disciples worried about feeding the crowd. They checked to see if anyone had food to share. All they found were five loaves of bread and two fish.

Jesus thanked God for the food and divided it between the disciples. They broke off chunks for each person. Everyone got enough to eat, and when they had finished, the disciples even collected twelve baskets of leftovers! Five loaves of bread and two fish had miraculously fed 5,000 people!

Another time, Jesus had been teaching on a hillside for three days. The baskets of food that people had brought were almost gone. Jesus did not want His followers to go hungry, so He asked the disciples to collect whatever food was left. They found only seven loaves of bread and a few small fish. Just as before, Jesus gave thanks to God and divided up the food. That day, He fed 4,000 people, with seven baskets remaining after everyone had eaten.

What was the Transfiguration?

Soon Jesus took Peter, James and John with Him to a quiet mountaintop. When they bowed to pray, Jesus' face grew as bright as the sun. Even his clothes began to glow. As the disciples watched, two men appeared — Moses and Elijah. They spoke to Jesus about His death on the cross. Then a cloud filled the sky, and a voice said, "This is My Son whom I love. Obey Him."

When the cloud passed, Jesus was alone. He asked the disciples not to tell others about what they had seen. But for Peter, James and John, the Transfiguration was another sign that Jesus truly was the Son of God.

Did Jesus tell the disciples about His death on the cross?

The more Jesus spoke about God's love, the more He angered the religious leaders. For years, the priests had said that sacrifices and offerings were the way to please God. Jesus said that loving God in your heart was more important.

Jesus knew that the leaders wanted to get rid of Him. Several times, He talked to the disciples about His death on the cross. "The Son of Man will be given to evil men," He said. "They will kill Him, but on the third day He will be raised from death."

These words filled the disciples with sadness, but they did not understand what Jesus meant.

What advice did Jesus give the rich young ruler?

A wealthy young man came to see Jesus. "Rabbi, what should I do to live forever?"

Jesus told the man to keep the Commandments: "Do not kill, do not steal, do not lie. Honor your parents, love your neighbors."

"I have obeyed all these laws," the young man said.

"Give your possessions to those who have nothing. Hand over your money to the poor. Then you will have treasure in heaven, and you can follow Me!" Jesus said.

The young man walked away sadly. It was too hard to give away all his nice things. His money meant more to him than God did.

Which are the greatest Commandments?

The Pharisees decided they would test Jesus to see if they could trap Him in a mistake. Surely they could make Jesus say something wrong about God. If He did, then they could put Him to death. One Pharisee was an expert in the Law of Moses. "Teacher," he asked Jesus, "of all the Commandments, which is the most important one?"

Jesus answered, "There are two: to love God with all your heart, soul and mind, and to love your neighbor as much as you love yourself. All the other laws depend on these two commands."

The Pharisees could find nothing wrong with Jesus' answer.

Who asked to sit beside Jesus in heaven?

Two of the disciples, James and John, came to Jesus with a special request. "Lord," they said, "let the two of us sit beside You, one on the left and one of the right, when You take Your place in heaven."

When the other disciples heard what James and John had asked, they grew angry. But Jesus told them all, "In my kingdom, the one who wants to be great must serve everyone else. If you want to be first, you must be willing to be last. That is the way of the Son of Man. He came to serve others. He came to give His life so that other people might live."

Who were Mary and Martha?

Mary and Martha lived with their brother Lazarus in the village of Bethany near Jerusalem. Their home was a favorite stopping spot for Jesus because He loved this family. One day Martha was hard at work preparing special dishes for Jesus when she realized her sister was not helping. Instead, Mary sat at Jesus' feet, listening to His words. Martha became angry. "Lord, tell Mary to help me! There is much work to do!"

Jesus gently reminded Martha not to worry so much about unimportant things. Mary had chosen to listen and learn, Jesus said, and that should not be taken away from her.

Why were caves used for tombs in ancient times?

During Bible times, people used caves for tombs because it was quicker and easier than digging a hole in the stony soil. Due to the warm climate, a dead body was buried as soon as possible. It was rubbed with spices and wrapped in cloth, then placed in the cave. A large boulder would close off the opening to prevent anyone from disturbing the body. After many months had passed, family members would re-open the cave, and place the bones in a special jar. The tomb would then be ready to use again.

Why did Jesus raise Lazarus from the dead?

Lazarus, the brother of Mary and Martha, was one of Jesus' good friends. Lazarus became ill, and his sisters sent word to Jesus that He come and heal him. When Jesus heard their message, He told the disciples, "Lazarus' illness will not end in death. It will show the glory of God."

By the time Jesus reached the home of Mary and Martha, Lazarus had already died and been placed in the tomb. Jesus ordered that the stone be removed. Martha said, "But Lord, it has been four days. Lazarus' body will smell bad."

Jesus answered, "If you believe, you will see the glory of God." Jesus then commanded Lazarus to come out. Still wearing the burial cloths, Lazarus stepped out of the cave, alive!

When the priests heard what Jesus had done, they made plans to arrest Him.

When did Jesus enter Jerusalem riding on a donkey?

For almost three years, Jesus had been teaching about God. From the smallest village to the very courtyard of the Temple, people everywhere spoke of Jesus and His miraculous works.

As the time of Passover neared, Jesus and the disciples made plans to go to Jerusalem to celebrate. The news spread throughout the city - Jesus was coming! People quickly lined the road. As Jesus entered the gate riding on a donkey, a great shout went up. "Hosanna! Praise to the Son of David! Blessed is the One who comes in the name of the Lord!"

Some people waved palm branches; some even threw their coats down on the road so Jesus would not get dusty. For one brief moment, they treated Jesus like a king.

Why did Jesus cry for Jerusalem?

Jesus watched people's faces as He rode through the city of Jerusalem. Even though the crowds were cheering, Jesus knew most of the people would choose not to believe His words. Love and sadness filled Jesus' heart: "Jerusalem, Jerusalem! The time is coming when your enemies will destroy you! Not one stone of your buildings will be left on top of another. And here is the reason why: when God came to save you, you did not know it."

How did the religious leaders try to trap Jesus?

Many people had come to Jerusalem to celebrate Passover, and Jesus continued to preach. The priests who heard His words tried to trap Him with difficult questions about God's ways. Over and over, they gave Him problems that would be hard for the most learned Bible scholar to solve. But no matter what they asked, Jesus' answers amazed them. Not once did He speak a word unworthy of His Heavenly Father.

What did Jesus think of the religious leaders?

Jesus called them hypocrites. He said. "You leaders make strict rules for the people to follow, but you do not keep them yourselves. You are careful to give God one-tenth of everything you own, even down to the tiny plants in your gardens. But you do not obey the most important laws: being fair, showing kindness, forgiving others. You are like a person who picks a fly out of his cup and then swallows a camel! You worry about a little mistake but a big sin does not bother you.

"Woe unto you! The kingdom of God will be taken from you. It will be given to people who do the things that God wants. You know what the Scriptures say: 'The stone that the builders did not want became the cornerstone.'"

Jesus said this so the leaders would know He was the cornerstone described in the Old Testament.

Where did Jesus eat the Last Supper?

Jerusalem was packed with visitors who had come to celebrate Passover. All the inns were full of people making preparations for the traditional meal. The disciples asked Jesus, "Lord, where shall we go?"

Jesus sent Peter and John to look for a man carrying a water jar. "Follow him to the house where he goes. Tell the owner that I want to celebrate Passover there."

Everything happened just as Jesus said. Peter and John brought food for the Passover meal to an upper room in a follower's home.

Why did Jesus wash the disciples' feet?

That evening, when the disciples arrived at the upper room, they were amazed to see Jesus remove His outer clothing. He wrapped a towel around His waist, poured water into a bowl, and began washing the disciples' dusty feet.

"Lord," Peter exclaimed, "You are our Master. You should not do the work of a servant!"

Jesus answered, "Yes, Peter, I am your Lord and Master, and I have washed your feet. Follow my example; serve one another. A servant is not greater than his master. A messenger is not greater than the one who sent him."

By washing the disciples' feet, Jesus showed us that we should help other people, no matter how dirty the job.

What did the food served at the Last Supper symbolize?

Flat bread and wine were always served at Passover. The bread reminded the Jews of the time they had left Egypt quickly, without enough time for dough to rise. At the Last Supper, however, Jesus gave flat bread and wine a new meaning.

"I wanted very much to eat this meal with you," Jesus told His disciples. "I will not eat again until God's plan is finished." Then He gave thanks, and broke off pieces of bread. "This is My body which I am giving for you. Eat, and remember Me."

Then Jesus took a cup of wine, gave thanks to God, and passed it around. "Drink, all of you. This cup symbolizes the new promise God makes with all people. It begins with My blood, which is poured out for you."

What did Judas plan to do?

While Peter and John had been preparing the Passover meal, the disciple Judas had also been busy. He had gone to see the leading priests and soldiers at the Temple. Judas knew the religious leaders wanted to capture Jesus, and he offered to turn his Master over to them in a quiet place, where the crowds would not see. Pleased that one of Jesus' very own disciples would help them, the priests offered Judas a large sum of money if he could do as he promised.

Did Jesus know what Judas planned to do?

As the disciples were eating together in the upper room, Jesus quietly said, "One of you will turn against Me."

The men wondered at His words. Who could ever do this to Jesus? But Judas looked up in amazement.

"What you are about to do, do quickly," Jesus said. And Judas slipped out of the room. The others simply thought he was running an errand for Jesus.

What did Peter promise at the Last Supper?

Jesus tried to tell the disciples about the terrible hours that were coming, His trial and death on the cross. "My children, I will be with you only a little longer. Where I go, you cannot come."

Peter replied, "Lord, I will go anywhere with You. I am even ready to die for You!"

Jesus looked sadly at His beloved disciple. "Peter, before the rooster crows three times tonight, you will pretend you don't know Me!"

As Peter looked puzzled, another disciple spoke up. "Lord, we don't know where You are going. How can we know the way?"

"I am the way, the truth and the life," Jesus said. "The only way to God is by knowing Me. I am going to prepare a place for you in My Father's house. But I will not leave you all alone. The Father will send the Holy Spirit to be with you until I return."

Why did Jesus go to the Garden of Gethsamene?

After sharing the Passover meal, Jesus and his disciples went to the Garden of Gethsamene. It was a beautiful spot high on a hill called the Mount of Olives. Jesus had often gone there to pray, and on this night He went off a short way to be alone.

He knelt down and prayed, "Do not let me go through the suffering of death on the cross. But Father, do what you want, not what I want."

Jesus was filled with pain. Drops of sweat fell from his face. And God sent an angel from heaven to comfort Him.

Who lost an ear in Gethsamene?

As Jesus and the disciples prayed, Judas led the Temple soldiers to the Garden. He rushed up and kissed Jesus on the cheek, so the soldiers would know which man to arrest.

Two of the disciples had brought swords with them; they tried to protect their Master. As they struck at the soldiers, Peter cut off the ear of Malchus, the servant of the high priest.

"No!" Jesus cried. All confusion stopped at that moment. Jesus lifted His hand to the servant's ear and healed it. Then He calmly allowed the soldiers to take Him.

The disciples ran away.

Where did the religious leaders take Jesus?

As the Temple soldiers led Jesus through the streets of Jerusalem, He said, "Do you think I am a crook? I was in the Temple every day. You could have come for Me there. But you came by night. You belong to the darkness."

The soldiers took Jesus to the house of Caiaphas, the high priest, where members of the Sanhedrin had secretly gathered. Under the cover of darkness, they questioned Jesus and argued all night. They wanted to silence Jesus without angering the crowds who had welcomed Him to Jerusalem.

What was the Sanhedrin?

The Sanhedrin was a council of priests who guided the Jewish people in following the Law of Moses. They held trials to decide what was right and wrong according to the Scriptures. In Jesus' day, when Rome ruled the land, the powers of the Sanhedrin were limited. Although they could put Jesus on trial, they were not allowed to condemn Him to death. Only the Roman leaders could make that decision.

Why did the high priest tear his clothes at Jesus' trial?

As he questioned Jesus, Caiaphas grew angry. After months of preaching against the priests and Pharisees, Jesus made no effort to defend Himself! So Caiaphas asked one more question: "By the power of the Living God, tell us the truth. Are You the Son of God?"

The religious leaders gasped. They knew Jesus had not committed any crime. He certainly was a gifted teacher who knew the Law of Moses well. He might even be the Messiah; the man chosen by God to lead Israel to peace. But what human being could ever claim to be son of the Most High God of Heaven?

Jesus did. He said, "Yes, I am the Son of God. One day you will see Me sitting at His right hand."

Caiaphas tore his clothes in rage. Other priests spit in Jesus' face and hit Him with their fists. This was blasphemy! This was an insult to the Lord! No one could claim to be as great as God! For this, Jesus must die!

What did Judas' betrayal money buy?

When Judas realized that the chief priests intended to kill Jesus, he was filled with despair. He tried to return the money he had been paid, but the priests would not take it. Judas threw the coins on the Temple floor. No one would touch them; they had paid for a man's death. Judas rushed out and hanged himself.

Later, the leaders used the money to buy a plot of land where they could bury strangers who died while visiting Jerusalem. The spot was named Aceldama, Field of Blood.

Which disciple pretended he did not know Jesus?

As Caiaphas questioned Jesus, Peter slipped into the courtyard and hid in the night shadows. The disciple had not been brave enough to stay with his Master, but now he wanted to know what was going on. A servant girl recognized Peter: "You are one of Jesus' men, aren't you?"

"No," Peter mumbled. "I don't know what you're talking about."

Another servant spoke up. "Yes, I remember him. He is one of Jesus' followers."

A third person said, "Listen to his country accent. He came from Nazareth with Jesus!"

Peter cursed that he did not know Jesus, and off in the distance, a rooster crowed. Jesus' words about Peter had come true. The disciple ran away and cried.

Who was Pontius Pilate?

The religious leaders did not have the power to put Jesus to death, so they took Him to the Roman governor.

Angry voices woke Pontius Pilate early. He patiently listened as the religious leaders accused Jesus of stirring up trouble, of making problems for Rome. The man standing calmly before him certainly did not look very dangerous. So Pilate asked, "Are you the king of the Jews?"

Jesus answered, "I am. My kingdom does not belong to this world. I was born to tell people the truth. Anyone who knows the truth belongs to My kingdom."

Who was Barabbas?

By the time Pilate had finished questioning Jesus, a large crowd had gathered outside the building. The very same people who had welcomed Jesus with palm branches now shouted ugly words. They had hoped Jesus would lead them in battle against the Romans, but he didn't.

Pilate heard their shouts and did not know what to do. So he said to the people, "I can find no crime in Jesus. But I will set one prisoner free because of Passover. Who do you want – Jesus or Barabbas the Robber?

The crowd chose Barabbas.

What did Pilate's wife dream?

As Pilate thought about what to do with Jesus, his wife sent him a message. The message said, "Today I dreamed that this man Jesus is not guilty. Do not harm him. I am afraid because of this dream."

But when the crowd began shouting for Jesus' death, Pilate forgot about his wife's warning. The Bible does not mention her again.

How did the Roman soldiers make fun of Jesus?

Pilate ordered his guards to beat Jesus. They used whips which were very heavy, with metal tips. Men often died from this type of beating. Jesus was badly hurt, but He did not die.

Then the soldiers wrapped Jesus in a red coat. They made a crown from thorny branches and jammed it roughly on His head. Drops of blood trickled down his face. "Look!" they laughed. "It's the King of the Jews! Hail, O King!" The soldiers bowed before Jesus to make fun of Him. Then they spit on Him and beat Him again with sticks.

Why did Pilate wash his hands at Jesus' trial?

After his soldiers had beaten Jesus, Pilate brought Him out once more before the crowd. "What shall I do with this Jesus, who has done no wrong?" he asked.

The crowd screamed, "Kill Him on a cross! Our law says He should die because He claims to be the Son of God."

When Pilate saw the crowd was against him, he took water and made a show of washing his hands. "I am not guilty of this man's death," he said. "You are to blame."

Who carried the cross when Jesus stumbled?

The soldiers led Jesus away from Pilate's palace and placed a heavy wooden beam on His back. "March!" came the order, and Jesus began the long walk through the streets of Jerusalem. The beam on His back was very heavy; He was weak from the beatings; people yelled curses and threw trash every step of the way. At last Jesus stumbled and fell, unable to carry His own cross.

The soldiers grabbed a man from the crowd. His name was Simon, and he was a visitor in Jerusalem. "Here, you! Pick up that cross and follow us!"

Simon carried Jesus' cross the rest of the way to the place where criminals were put to death.

Where was Jesus crucified?

The Gospel writers tell us that Jesus was taken outside the city walls of Jerusalem to be executed. His cross was probably raised alongside a road, because we read that people walked by and insulted Jesus as He hung there. The spot may have been on a rocky hillside near caves used for burial, for Jesus' friends carried His body to the tomb before sundown. Two different names are given for this spot, Calvary and Golgotha. Both names mean The Place of the Skull.

Why was crucifixion such a horrible punishment?

Death on a cross was a Roman punishment, reserved for the worst criminals. It was a slow painful way to die, usually taking two or three days. The person's hands were tied or nailed to the cross in a position that made it hard to breathe deeply. The feet were placed on a peg and fastened there. As long as the person had strength, he could push himself up on the peg and take a good breath. As he grew tired, he took in less and less air, eventually dying from lack of oxygen. To bring death more quickly, a victim's legs would sometimes be broken.

What sign was placed on Jesus' cross?

After the Roman soldiers put Jesus on the cross, they continued to make fun of Him. First, they made a sign: "Here is the King of the Jews." They nailed it on the cross above Jesus' head. Then they gambled to see which one of them would get to keep His clothes. And when Jesus asked them for a drink, they held up a sponge dipped in vinegar.

What promise did Jesus make to the dying thief?

Now on that same day, Pilate's soldiers brought two other men to Calvary to execute them. They hung one criminal on the right side of Jesus, the other on the left. As the crowd shouted insults at Jesus, one of the criminals joined in: "Aren't you supposed to be the Messiah? Then save yourself - and us, too!"

The other criminal, who was a robber, stopped him. "Don't you fear God even now that you are dying? We are getting the punishment we deserve. But this man has done nothing wrong." Then the thief looked into Jesus' eyes. It was as if time stood still for a moment. Perfect peace and love seemed to shine from Jesus' face. "Jesus," he said, "when You get to Your kingdom, remember me!"

Jesus answered him, "I tell you the truth. Today you will be with Me in paradise!"

How did Jesus care for his mother from the cross?

The hours passed slowly. Jesus grew weaker and weaker. His head drooped on His chest and His eyes closed. But at the sound of women crying, He looked out. There at the foot of the cross stood His mother Mary. With her were others that Jesus loved dearly: Mary Magdalene, Mary the wife of Clopas, and the young disciple John. Of all the followers, only these few came to weep at Jesus' feet.

Jesus spoke to Mary. "Dear mother, from now on, John will be like a son to you."

Then He looked at His disciple. "Treat her like your own mother, John."

From that time on, John took Mary to live with him in his home.

What were Jesus' last words before He died?

Since early morning, Jesus had suffered on the cross. Around noontime, a great darkness fell over the city of Jerusalem. Jesus lifted His head to heaven, eyes wide open in fear, and cried, "My God, My God! Why have You forsaken me?" Matthew 27:46

Three more hours went by. Those still watching by the cross had not seen Jesus move at all for most of that time. Suddenly, He cried out in a loud voice, "Father, I give You my life. It is finished."

And Jesus died.

What happened the moment when Jesus died?

An army officer standing guard at the cross saw Jesus die. "Truly, this was a good man," he told his men. Just then, the earth began to shake. Rocks broke apart. The soldiers were frightened and grabbed one another as they ran away. "Jesus really was the Son of God!" they exclaimed.

All through Jerusalem strange things happened the moment Jesus died. At the Temple, the curtain in front of the inner holy room tore from top to bottom. Tombs opened, and dead people came back to life. They walked through the city and many people saw them. For a time all the city was in chaos.

Why did soldiers stab Jesus' body?

When at last the earth stopped rumbling, the soldiers came back to check on the men hanging at Calvary. The two criminals were still alive, so the soldiers broke their legs. This would bring death more quickly.

But when they saw that Jesus already looked dead, they did not break His legs. Instead, a soldier stuck his spear in Jesus' side, just to make sure He was not alive. All these things happened just as predicted.

Who provided a tomb and spices for Jesus' body?

In the crowd at Calvary that day were many members of the Sanhedrin. They watched as the Roman soldiers carried out the order to crucify Jesus. Two from the council had secretly become His followers: Nicodemus and Joseph of Arimathea.

The other men of the Sanhedrin were amazed as these two lovingly lifted Jesus' body down from the cross. Joseph was a wealthy merchant and owned a tomb nearby. Nicodemus brought 75 pounds of burial spices - enough for a king. Together, they took the body and wrapped it with the spices in pieces of cloth.

Nicodemus and Joseph, along with other followers, hurried to place the body in the tomb before sundown, when the Sabbath would begin. According to Jewish law, no work was permitted on that day. They did not have time to finish preparing Jesus' body before dark, so they laid it in the cave and rolled a large rock over the opening. Several women planned to return the day after the Sabbath, to complete the preparations.

Why did the high priest post guards at the tomb?

When Jesus died, the priests and Pharisees suddenly remembered what He had said: that He would rise from death after three days. So they went again to Pilate. "Sir, you must post guards by Jesus' tomb until three days have passed. Otherwise, His followers might steal the body and tell people He has risen."

So Pilate sent soldiers to guard the cave where Jesus had been placed.

Who discovered that Jesus' tomb was empty?

At dawn, the day after the Sabbath, Mary Magdalene and two other women went to the tomb to finish wrapping Jesus' body. From a long way off Mary could see that something was wrong - the stone had been moved from the opening of the cave. She ran and looked inside. Jesus' body was gone! The tomb was empty! How could anyone be mean enough to steal a dead body?
Mary began to cry.

Suddenly she heard a voice close behind her. "Lady," the voice asked softly, "why are you crying?"

Mary whirled around. It was Jesus. He was alive. He had risen from the dead, just as He had promised. Mary knelt at Jesus' feet and worshipped Him.

"Don't be afraid, Mary," Jesus said. "Go and tell my brothers everything that you have seen."

Mary ran to the place where the disciples had gathered. She told them what had happened at the tomb. But the men did not believe her.

When did the risen Jesus appear to his disciples?

When Peter heard Mary's words, he ran to see the tomb for himself. Except for the crumpled burial cloth, the tomb was empty. Peter wandered off, deep in thought: What had happened?

That evening, as some of the disciples were eating supper in a locked room, Jesus suddenly came to them. "Peace be with you," He said.

For a long moment, no one moved. Could this really be Jesus, alive? Or were they seeing a ghost?

Jesus smiled. "Don't be afraid! Look at My hands and feet. You can see for yourselves that I have a living body. I am hungry, too. Share some of your food with Me!"

Jesus spent the evening with His disciples, explaining why He had to die on the cross. He opened their minds and at last they began to understand God's plan.

Which disciple is called The Doubting One?

Thomas was not with the other disciples the night that Jesus first appeared. No matter what the others said, Thomas did not believe them. Jesus was dead! He had seen the lifeless body with his own eyes. He said, "I will never believe until I see the nail marks in Jesus' hands, until I get to touch them myself."

Suddenly, Jesus stood before him, holding out His hands. "Thomas, put your finger here. Then touch the wound on My side. Stop doubting, and believe in Me!"

Who met Jesus on the road to Emmaus?

On this same day, two of Jesus' followers left Jerusalem to go to Emmaus, a town about seven miles away. Another traveler joined them and asked what they were talking about. The followers told him of Jesus' death, and that His tomb was empty.

The stranger said, "Don't you remember? The prophets said this would happen!" And the man began to explain all that the Scriptures said about the Christ.

When it came time to stop for supper, the followers invited the stranger to eat with them. He took the bread and gave thanks for it. Instantly, the followers realized it was Jesus Himself who had been walking with them!

Why did Jesus tell Peter to feed His sheep?

Later Jesus showed Himself to his disciples as they were fishing in the Sea of Galilee. After they pulled in a huge catch of fish and ate them, Jesus turned to Peter. "Do you love Me, Peter?" He asked.

Peter answered, "Yes, Lord! You know that I love You!"

"Then feed My sheep," Jesus said.

Twice more that night, Jesus told Peter to take care of His lambs. Finally Peter understood. Jesus would be going back to heaven soon, and all the new believers needed someone to take care of them. Jesus wanted Peter to be their shepherd.

How was Jesus taken up to heaven?

After the disciples had been with Jesus for forty days, He led them to a mountain top. The disciples realized Jesus was going to leave them.

"Do not be sad," Jesus said. "I go to My Father now so that the Holy Spirit can come to you. Then you will receive power to tell everyone about Me – in Jerusalem, in Judea, in Samaria, in all the world!"

As the disciples watched, Jesus was lifted into the air and hidden by a cloud.

What is the Great Commission?

The Gospel of Matthew ends with Jesus' last words to His disciples, spoken just before He returned to heaven. Jesus was like a commander ordering soldiers to carry out an important mission. When we read His words, we realize Jesus was speaking to all believers, not just those first disciples.

Go ye therefore, and teach all nations, baptizing them in the name of the Father, and of the Son, and of the Holy Ghost: teaching them to observe all things whatsoever I have commanded you; and lo, I am with you always, even unto the end of the world.

What is Pentecost?

Pentecost is the day when the Holy Spirit came to give the disciples power after Jesus' resurrection.

The disciples were together in Jerusalem when they heard a noise like a strong wind. Over their heads flames of fire appeared, and they were filled with the Holy Spirit. Suddenly each man began to speak in a different language, telling of the great things God had done. A large crowd gathered to listen. "How can this be?" people asked. "These men are from Galilee, yet they speak the language of every foreigner here today!"

Who gave his first sermon at Pentecost?

At Pentecost, many people thought the disciples were drunk. "Those men have just had too much wine!" they laughed.

But Peter stood up. "People of Jerusalem, listen! We are not drunk; we are full of God's spirit! God did miracles, signs, and wonders through Jesus, but you killed Him. God knew this would happen. He raised Jesus from death and made Him Lord and Christ. King David, our ancestor, knew about this plan. So change your hearts and lives! Repent of your sins and be baptised in Jesus' name. Then you will receive the same Holy Spirit that is in us."

Three thousand people believed in Jesus because of Peter's sermon that day.

What were the early Christians like?

The good news that Jesus had risen from death spread. More and more people came to listen to the disciples, and many became believers. They wanted to be together, so they found places to live near one another. The believers sold the things they owned and gave the money to the poor. They shared meals with anyone who was hungry. Every day they met in the Temple to worship God together.

People liked the believers because they were good and kind. The Lord blessed them with new members every day.

Who was Gamaliel?

Gamaliel was a well-known teacher and a member of the Sanhedrin. The disciples were spreading the news that Jesus had risen from the dead, and the leaders wanted to kill them. Gamaliel voted no. This was not because he believed in Jesus. "Do not kill these men," Gamaliel said. "If this plan comes from their own minds, it will fail all by itself. But if it comes from God, we can do nothing to stop it. We do not want to be guilty of fighting against God!"

Even though the disciples were beaten for speaking about Jesus, they did not stop, and the good news traveled far.

Who restored Dorcas to life?

Dorcas was one of the first Christians in the city of Joppa. A poor woman herself, she made clothes for widows who were left with nothing. When Dorcas became sick and died, the other Christians in Joppa sent word to the disciple Peter in Jerusalem. He came quickly, and found the widows weeping over her body. Peter sent them away. He prayed to God, and then told Dorcas to rise. Calling the widows back into the room, he showed them that their dear friend was alive again.

The news spread throughout the city, and many people believed in the Lord Jesus on that day.

Why did Peter dream of clean and unclean animals?

The smell of good cooking made Peter hungry! It was almost time for the noon meal, and he went up on the roof to pray. There God gave him a vision. Peter saw a big sheet being lowered down from heaven. In the sheet were all kinds of animals. A voice said, "Get up, Peter. Kill and eat." Peter drew back in horror. Some of the animals in the sheet were unclean – not good for man to eat. But then the voice said, "God has made all these animals clean."

This vision taught Peter that to God, every person is the same. He accepts everyone who loves and serves Him, Jew and Gentile alike.

Who was Cornelius?

Cornelius, an officer in the Roman army, was the first Gentile to become a believer. He lived in Caesarea where he had learned much about the God of Israel. One afternoon, an angel spoke to Cornelius: "Send for Peter."

It was against the religious laws for a Jew to visit a Gentile. But since Peter had seen the vision of the animals, he agreed to meet with Cornelius and his family. As he taught them about Jesus, the Holy Spirit came down. Peter turned to the Jewish believers with him. "Jesus did not come only for the Jews! These people have received the Holy Spirit just as we did. Truly, Jesus is the Lord of all people!"

Who was Paul?

Paul was the son of a Pharisee. He grew up in the city of Tarsus, in a country north of Judea. As a youth, he came to Jerusalem to study with the famous teacher Gamaliel. He became one of the smartest young men at the Temple.

Paul hated those Jews who believed in Jesus. He wanted to stop them from preaching – even if it meant killing them. Paul tracked down believers wherever they hid and punished them. Those first Christians feared Paul greatly, for he was very good at his job.

What happened on the road to Damascus?

Paul heard that many Jews in the city of Damascus believed in Jesus. He planned to find them and bring them back to Jerusalem to stand trial before the Sanhedrin.

But as he was on the road, a bright light suddenly flashed around him. Paul fell to the ground. A voice spoke. "Paul, Paul, why do you work against Me?"

Paul asked, "Who are you, sir?"

The voice answered, "I am Jesus, the One you are trying to hurt. Go to Damascus. I will send someone to you there."

The light vanished. Paul's men helped him up. He discovered that he could not see anything, so the men led him by the hand.

In Damascus, the Lord spoke to a believer named Ananias. He told him to visit Paul and heal his blindness. Ananias said, "Lord, I have heard terrible things about this man!"

God answered, "Go! I have chosen Paul for a very important job." So Ananias went and prayed with Paul. Something like fish scales fell from Paul's eyes, and he could see once more. Immediately, Paul got up and was baptized. From that day on, he worked to spread the good news about Jesus to all the world.

Where were Jesus' followers first called Christians?

Each day, more and more people came to believe in Jesus. The leaders ordered harsh punishments for any who accepted Him. Life in Jerusalem became too dangerous, so many believers moved to other cities. Some of them ended up in Antioch, a city in Syria. The church there grew to be the largest group of believers, and for the first time, people called them Christians.

How did Herod hurt the church?

King Herod always tried to keep the Temple leaders happy. When he saw how the priests hated the Christians, he ordered his soldiers to find the disciples. James, the brother of John, was captured and killed, and Peter was thrown in jail. The believers feared that Herod would also kill Peter, and they prayed for his safety. The night before his trial, an angel came to Peter's jail and his chains fell from his hands. Gates opened by themselves as the angel led Peter to freedom.

God's message continued to spread. More people became Christians every day.

Who was Barnabas?

Barnabas was the first person in the early church to recognize Paul's great future as a missionary to the Gentiles.

After meeting Jesus on the road to Damascus, Paul went home. For three years, he lived a quiet life, learning from the Holy Spirit. While other church leaders remained suspicious of Paul's new faith, Barnabas encouraged him. He invited Paul to go with him on a journey to preach the Gospel. Many people believed because of that trip.

Later, Paul and Barnabas split up, each man taking the message of Jesus Christ in different directions. Without the encouragement and friendship of Barnabas, Paul might not ever have undertaken his great work of preaching to the Gentile world.

How did Paul and Silas heal a fortune-teller?

For his second missionary trip, Paul chose a man named Silas to travel with him. They went throughout Turkey and Greece, telling all who would listen about the Lord Jesus.

In Philippi, they met a servant girl who was famous for predicting the future. She could do this because there was an evil spirit in her. People paid money to listen to her wild words. When Paul and Silas commanded the spirit to leave, the servant instantly became a normal, happy young woman. But her owners were furious -- who would pay money to listen to her now?

How did Priscilla and Aquila help Paul?

Paul met Priscilla and Aquila in the city of Corinth. Like Paul, they were tent-makers; they cut and stitched hides for merchants, travelers, and shepherds. They were also Christians and helped their dear friend Paul in many ways. They gave him work so he could earn money, they traveled to spread the word of God, and they held church meetings at their house. Paul loved this couple and sent greetings to them in his letters.

How did Paul teach the people of Athens about God?

When Paul reached the city of Athens, he saw that the people were very religious. They worshipped every god they heard about and made many idols. They were so afraid of leaving out an important god, they even built an extra altar and put a sign over it: "To the god we do not know yet."

Paul pointed to this altar. "People of Athens, I want to tell you about this very God. He is the God who made the world and everything in it. He has always loved you, even though you did not know about Him."

Paul went on to explain that God sent Jesus to earth so people could see and understand Him. If people would believe in Him, they would not need to worship any other gods. Many in Athens laughed at Paul, but some became Christians.

Who were the seven sons of Sceva?

Paul spent two years in the Asian city of Ephesus. There God blessed him with extra power. Even his clothes and handkerchiefs were filled with God's healing spirit. People took them and placed them on others who were sick. Their illnesses would be healed, just from a touch of Paul's clothing.

But other men in Ephesus also claimed to have this power. Seven sons of a priest named Sceva tried to heal in Jesus' name, even though they did not believe in Him. An evil spirit living in a sick man said to them, "I know Jesus. I know Paul. But who are you?" Then the evil spirit left the sick man and attacked the sons of Sceva. All who saw feared and honored the Lord.

Who was "almost persuaded" to believe in Jesus?

The leaders hated Paul. In many cities, Paul was put in jail. Finally he was arrested and brought before Agrippa, the king of Judea and Samaria. Agrippa had already heard much about Jesus. He was curious to hear what Paul would say.

Paul preached a simple sermon. He told the story of his own life, first as one who hated Jesus, and then as one who told the truth about Him. Agrippa was impressed. "Paul, you have almost persuaded even me to become a Christian!" he exclaimed.

How did a Roman soldier show kindness to Paul?

The book of Acts tells the story of Julius, the army officer given the job of guarding Paul while he was under arrest. Paul and some other prisoners were sent to Rome on a ship. When the ship stopped at a city along the way, Paul's guard kindly allowed him to visit friends for a few hours.

Several days later, a terrible storm wrecked the ship on a sandbar. Some of the soldiers wanted to kill the prisoners so they would not escape. But Julius ordered everyone, even the prisoners, to swim to safety. Floating on pieces of the wrecked ship, Paul and all the other passengers made it safely to land.

Why did the people of Malta believe Paul was a god?

Paul's ship had wrecked near the island of Malta. The people living there built a fire to warm the cold wet passengers. Paul helped by gathering sticks of wood. Suddenly a poisonous snake came out and bit Paul's hand. The people of Malta exclaimed, "This must be an evil man. First the sea tried to kill him and now this snake has bitten him!" And they waited for Paul to die. But nothing happened. The snake bite did not harm Paul at all. The islanders thought surely Paul was a god to have such power.

How did Paul spend his time in prison?

Paul spent at least two years under arrest in Rome. Although he was chained to a soldier night and day, he was allowed to live in his own house as he waited for his trial. Since Paul could not continue his journeys, he wrote letters and spoke to the many people who came to visit.

The Bible says that many of the soldiers assigned to guard Paul in Rome became Christians. Even with His missionary in prison, God caused the good news about Jesus to spread as the soldiers traveled through the Roman Empire.

What are the Epistles?

The word "epistle" means "letter." Many of the books in the New Testament are actually letters that Paul wrote to the early Christian churches. The new believers had no book to guide them, so Paul wrote about the real-life problems they faced. He taught them how to live so their lives would show Christ. The churches treasured these letters. People saved them to read over and over again. Even today, hundreds of years later, Paul's words still speak to us as we try to live God's way. Some of the Epistles are Ephesians, Galatians, Romans, 1st and 2nd Corinthians, Philippians and Colossians.

How did Paul die?

The Bible does not tell what happened to Paul after he was imprisoned in Rome. From other written records, we believe Paul was released two years later. He continued to travel, and may have taken the Word of God as far away as Spain. Later, Paul was put in prison again. He was beheaded sometime around the year 66 A.D. and buried in the caves of Rome.

Why is Paul called an apostle?

Paul was not one of the original twelve disciples. He never saw Jesus before His death and resurrection. But Paul knew Jesus' thoughts as well as any of the men who had been with Him for three years. When the risen Jesus appeared on the road to Damascus, it was as if Paul was getting a new heart and a new mind filled only with Christ.

The word "apostle" means "one who is sent off." Certainly this definition fits Paul, for he traveled thousands of miles and faced great hardship to spread the Gospel. The twelve disciples are also sometimes referred to as apostles.

How did Paul handle problems and suffering?

When Paul faced hardships in his life, he remembered the glory that waits for people who love God. He asked the Romans, "If God is for us, who can be against us? Can any problem separate us from the love of God? Suffering, danger, death, evil powers - nothing in the whole world will ever be able to separate us from the love of God that is in Christ Jesus our Lord!"

Who were Paul's friends in Rome?

Paul's letter to the Roman church closes with greetings to his friends. Paul listed the names of 25 people that he knew and loved in Rome. These were men and women who worked hard to serve the Lord. Everywhere Paul preached, he made friends. People loved him because he taught the truth about God. Several of Paul's other letters list even more names. Although Paul never got to spend much time with these friends, he loved them and prayed for them always. He thought of them as his brothers and sisters in Christ.

Who were the Corinthians?

When Paul wrote his two letters to the Corinthians, he was writing to dear friends. Paul himself started the church in Corinth, a large city in Greece. He went there and found work with Aquila and Priscilla, the tent-makers. For a year and a half, Paul lived in Corinth, teaching the people about Jesus Christ. It was a difficult job, for most of them worshipped the Greek gods. But the Lord was at work changing hearts, and the little group of believers grew larger and larger.

After Paul left Corinth, the Christians there struggled to live in ways that would please God. It seemed so hard! At last, they wrote to Paul and asked many questions. The Books of First and Second Corinthians were Paul's answer.

Why did Paul write about running a race?

Paul said that being a Christian was like being a runner. The believers in Corinth had seen many athletic events, so they understood what Paul meant.

It took lots of practice to be a good runner, and it wasn't always fun. Only the athletes with courage and determination reached the prize at the end of the race. The runner won a crown of leaves that soon wilted. But Christians will win a crown that will last forever. "So run to win!" Paul said.

Why was food offered to idols a problem for the Corinthians?

Almost everyone living in Corinth worshipped pagan gods. Farmers and shepherds brought their animals to the pagan temples to be blessed. That meant all the meat for sale in the markets had been offered to false idols. This worried the Corinthian Christians. If they ate this meat, were they worshipping the idols? Paul said no. He reminded them that there is only one God, that the blessings of the pagan priests meant nothing. But Paul also said if eating the meat upset other Christians, they should not eat it. He wrote, "If the food I eat makes my brother sin, I will stop eating meat."

Why did Paul say we are the body of Christ?

Some of the Corinthian Christians boasted about their spiritual gifts. They thought the gifts God had given them were better than the gifts He gave other people. Paul told them that all spiritual gifts are important to God.

The church is just like the human body, Paul wrote. The eye can't say to the hand, "I don't need you!" A foot cannot say, "I'm not as good as the hand. I'm not part of this body." God put all the parts together to make one working body. That's how it is with the church, one body – the body of Christ.

What are Paul's famous words about love?

The book of 1st Corinthians contains one of the best-known passages in the New Testament. It is Paul's beautiful poem about love. Paul was sad to hear that the Corinthians were boasting about their spiritual gifts. They could have great abilities, Paul wrote, but without love, they had nothing. They could have enough faith to move mountains, and give all they owned to the poor. They could even offer their bodies as burnt sacrifices, but it would mean nothing unless they loved each other.

Love is patient, love is kind.
Love is not jealous, it does not brag, and it is not proud.
Love is not rude, is not selfish, and does not become angry easily.
Love does not remember wrongs done against it.
Love is not happy with evil, but is happy with truth.
Love bears all things, believes all things, hopes all things,
        endures all things.
Love never fails.

Three things will last forever: faith, hope, and love.
But the greatest of these is love.

What kinds of questions did people ask Paul?

People in Bible times were no different than people today. They wondered about death just as we do. The Corinthian Christians asked Paul how our bodies of skin and bone could be brought back to life in heaven. Paul's answer was that there are two bodies: a physical one and a spiritual one.

He wrote that dying is like planting a seed in the ground. The seed changes and grows into something far greater. When we die, our earthly bodies are "planted," but they will be raised as glorious spiritual bodies.

The Corinthians also wondered about sickness and growing old. Paul explained that while our physical bodies grow weaker, our spirits inside us are made new again every day. While we live on this earth, we will have sickness and problems, but they help us gain eternal glory. Paul wrote, "So we always have courage. We know that while we live in this body, we are away from the Lord. Our only goal is to please God, whether we are living here on earth or in heaven with Him."

What hardships did Paul endure?

Paul never complained about the difficulty of spreading the Gospel. But in the Book of 2nd Corinthians, he listed the hardships he had faced: prison, shipwrecks, whippings, beatings, stoning, thieves, hunger, bad weather, going without sleep, and more. "If I must boast," he said, "I will boast of the things that show my weakness, because they show the power of Christ in me."

Paul told about the time he was almost arrested in Damascus. His friends hid him in a basket. Later that night, they lowered the basket down the city wall so Paul could escape to freedom.

What was Paul's "thorn in the flesh?"

When we read about Paul's great missionary work, we think of him as a super Christian, strong in heart, mind and body. But Paul was human like the rest of us, and for many years he struggled with a problem that he called his "thorn in the flesh." Right after God allowed Paul to see incredible visions, this problem began bothering him. Paul wrote that he prayed three different times for God to take it away. The Lord chose to leave the problem with Paul.

Perhaps it was an illness or a handicap. It may have been sinful thoughts that bothered Paul. Whatever it was, Paul said it always reminded him that he was just an ordinary man working for an incredible God.

How can a Christian be a letter to the world?

"You are a letter from Christ, written not with ink but with the Spirit of the living God. . ." —II Corinthians 3:3

Paul spent countless hours writing to new churches. But there are letters much more important than the ones Paul wrote. The best letters are living letters, believers themselves. People may not study the Bible, but they can study the lives of the Christians around them.

What was Paul's message to the Galatians?

Paul traveled to Galatia, an area that is now the country of Turkey. There he won many Gentiles to Christ. But other teachers came behind Paul. They confused the Galatians by telling them they had to follow the Jewish laws before they could become Christians. What a lot of work that meant, learning hundreds of Old Testment rules!

Paul wrote a powerful letter to the Galatian churches. He said work would never make us right with God. We are saved by faith, not by works.

Why did Paul meet with Peter, James, and John?

In the book of Galatians, Paul tells of his meeting with the leaders of the early church. Most of the first Christians were Jewish. Even though Jesus came for all people, it was hard for the Jewish Christians to reach out to the Gentiles. Paul knew God had called him for this very job. So he went to Peter, James and John, to get their blessing before he began his missionary journeys. The disciples saw that God had indeed given Paul a special gift and encouraged him in his work.

What is the fruit of the Spirit?

"Do not be deceived: God is not mocked. A man reaps what he sows."
—Galatians 6:7

Paul used farming words in his letter to the Galatians. They were country folks; they knew a crop was only as good as the seed they planted. It is the same way with life; you cannot cheat God, Paul said. If you plant only to please your sinful self, sooner or later, your harvest will be sin. But if you plant to please the Holy Spirit, you will have a harvest that will last forever: Love, joy, peace, patience, kindness, goodness, faithfulness, gentleness, and self-control.

Who were the Ephesians?

The Ephesians of Paul's letter lived in the most important city in Asia. People came from all over to worship at the temple of the Roman goddess Diana. Because of its size and beauty, the temple was called one of the seven wonders of the world.

After Paul had preached in Ephesus for a time, the silver workers of the city grew angry. Demetrius, their leader, cried, "Men, you know we make much money selling small statues of Diana. But look at this man Paul! He says that the gods we make are not real. Soon no one will believe in Diana, and our business will die!" The silversmiths started a huge riot, so Paul left town.

Later, while he was in prison, Paul sent a letter to the Ephesian Christians. Remembering the beautiful temple of Diana, Paul wrote about God's church, made not of stone, but of changed hearts:

> You are no longer strangers, but members of God's house, built on the foundation of the apostles and prophets, with Christ Jesus Himself as the chief cornerstone. In Him the whole building is joined together and rises to become a holy temple in the Lord, a dwelling in which God lives by his Spirit.
>
> —Ephesians 2:19 – 22

What kind of spiritual armor did Paul write about?

Paul told his friends in Ephesus to put on the whole armor of God. Then they would be able to stand firm against the evil that is in the world.

"Wear a belt of truth around your waist. Put on the chest protector of righteousness. On your feet wear the good news about God's peace, and carry a shield of faith. Cover your head with the helmet of salvation and take the sword of the Spirit wherever you go."

Which is Paul's letter of joy?

Paul talks about joy sixteen times in his short letter to the Philippians. "Rejoice in the Lord always. Again I say, rejoice!"

Philippi was a large city in Macedonia. Most of the Christians there were poor, but they sent Paul a gift of money and clothing. The book of Philippians is Paul's thank-you letter, and it overflows with happiness.

Paul told his friends that the secret to happiness was knowing Jesus. He said, "I have learned to be happy when I have plenty to eat and when I am hungry. I have learned to be happy when I have all that I need and when I don't have what I need. I can do all things through Christ who strengthens me."

Who was Lydia?

Lydia was a member of the church in Philippi. She was a well-to-do merchant and sold fine purple cloth. The believers used her home for their meeting place.

When Paul first traveled to Philippi, he met Lydia and her friends down by a river. The women always gathered there to pray. Paul taught them about Jesus, and soon baptized Lydia. She invited Paul to stay at her house while he preached in Philippi. When Paul left, it may have been Lydia's idea to send money to help with his work.

What kind of clothing did Paul write about?

Paul used the idea of clothing in his letter to the Christians of Collose, a city in what is now Turkey. He compared living a good life to putting on new clothes: "Therefore, as God's chosen people, clothe yourselves with kindness, gentleness, and patience. Bear with each other and forgive one another as God forgave you. And over all this put on love, which binds all these good things together." Paul saw the good deeds of a Christian's life as pieces of clothing, held together by a belt of love.

What does Paul say about Jesus' return?

When Jesus left the disciples to return to heaven, He gave them His promise, "I will come again." Ever since that day, people have watched for Jesus' return.

In the two letters Paul wrote to the people of Thessalonia, a city in Macedonia, he explained that before Jesus comes back, evil things will happen. Large numbers of people will turn away from God. They will be ruled by a leader who gets his power from Satan. But then Jesus Himself will come down from heaven with His angels. He will punish with fire those who do not obey God. Then there will be a loud command, and those believers who have died will rise from their graves. They will be joined in the air by the living believers and together, they will meet Jesus in the clouds, to be with Him forever.

When will this happen?

Some of the early Christians looked for Jesus to return right away. They were so sure it would be soon, they quit their jobs and waited. In First Thessalonians, Paul wrote, "Brothers, you know that the day the Lord comes again will be a surprise, like a thief that comes in the night."

No one can know for sure just when Jesus will return.

Who was Timothy?

Timothy was like a son to Paul. He grew up in the city of Lystra in Turkey, and heard about Jesus when Paul went there to preach. Along with his mother and grandmother, Lois and Eunice, Timothy became a Christian. When Paul returned to Lystra a few years later, he found Timothy had grown into a fine young man. Paul invited Timothy to travel with him on his missionary journeys.

Later, Paul left Timothy in charge of the church at Ephesus. The young man had to deal with many problems there. So Paul sent him two letters of advice. First and Second Timothy have served as guidebooks for church workers ever since.

What problems did Timothy face?

There were no church buildings during this time. Small groups of believers met in homes, each with its own pastor. Timothy had to make sure that all the pastors taught the true Gospel of Jesus Christ. It was so easy for false ideas to creep in.

Timothy felt timid about taking this important job. Paul wrote, "You are young, but do not let anyone treat you as if you are unimportant. Be an example to show the believers how to live. Show them with your words, your love, your faith, and your pure life. Remember to use the gift that God gave you!"

Which book is Paul's good-bye letter?

Paul's second letter to Timothy was written in a Roman dungeon. Paul had been imprisoned again for preaching about Jesus. He had presented his case to the evil Roman emperor Nero. Nero hated the Christians, so Paul did not expect to live. Second Timothy is Paul's good-bye letter to his "beloved son." He wrote, "My life is being given as an offering to God. The time has come for me to leave this life. I have fought the good fight. I have finished the race. I have kept the faith. Now, a crown is waiting for me, and for all those who have loved God."

Who was Titus?

On one of Paul's first missionary journeys, he met a young Greek man named Titus. Titus became a Christian and later served as an important leader of the early church. Titus was a good problem-solver. He first went to Corinth to help the Christians there settle differences of opinion. Much later, Paul asked Titus to work with the church on the island of Crete. There, false teachers were stirring up trouble. Paul wrote his friend a letter full of good advice. That letter is part of the New Testament, the Book of Titus.

Who was Onesimus?

Philemon was a Christian who lived in the city of Colosse. He owned a young slave named Onesimus who ran away. According to Roman law, when a runaway slave was found and returned to his master, he could be harshly beaten.

Onesimus ran and hid in Rome. Somehow, the young slave met Paul, who was under arrest and waiting for his trial. Onesimus became a Christian and a dear friend to Paul. He wanted to stay in Rome. But Paul knew that Onesimus should do the right thing and return to his master in Colosse. Paul wrote Philemon, asking him to welcome Onesimus back, not as a slave, but as a new brother in Christ.

What covenant did God make in the New Testament?

In the Old Testament, God made an agreement with Abraham and his descendants. They would worship only Him, and He would bless them and make them into a great nation. God told His people to offer sacrifices so their sins would be forgiven.

The writer of the New Testament Book of Hebrews explains that Jesus came as God's new covenant with His people: "So Christ was sacrificed once to take away the sins of many people."

What does it mean to have faith?

"Now faith is being sure of what we hope for; faith is being certain of what we do not see." —Hebrews 11:1

What advice did James give to Christians?

James was one of Jesus' brothers, a son of Mary and Joseph. At first, James did not accept Jesus as the Son of God, sent to save the world from sin. But later he believed, and became an important leader.

James' letter gives very practical advice about how to live a Christian life. Here are some of his teachings:

1. Respect all people, rich and poor alike. Never think that some are more important than others. You must show kindness to people, or God will not show kindness to you.

2. Check your tongue. We say we love God, but then we turn around and curse people. The tongue is full of poison that can kill. So watch what you say!

3. Do not brag about your wisdom. If you are truly wise, you will show it by living right.

4. Do not try to control life yourself. Be open to what God wants for your life.

5. Let your word be true. When you mean yes, say only "yes." Do not use the Lord's name to prove what you say.

6. In sickness, happiness, good times and bad, pray to God. When righteous people pray, great things happen.

How did Nero punish the early Christians?

Nero was the leader of the Roman Empire from 54 A. D. to 68 A. D. Although he only ruled for fourteen years, he is remembered as one of the most evil leaders in history. Nero killed anyone who stood in the way of what he wanted. By his command, hundreds of respected officials were executed. Nero even ordered the deaths of his wife and his mother.

The Romans disliked Christians because they would not join in wild celebrations to honor Rome's gods. Then a great fire broke out and destroyed much of the city. It is believed that Nero himself started the fire so he could build a new palace. But Nero pinned the blame on the Christians. As a result, hundreds of believers were tortured and burned to death.

Who wrote a letter to encourage those who suffered for Jesus' sake?

By this time, the disciple Peter was an old man. He had spent his life telling his fellow Jews about Jesus. Through the strength of the Holy Spirit, the rough young fisherman had grown gentle and patient and wise. He himself was often beaten and jailed for following Jesus, and he knew how to endure great suffering. In the letters known as 1st and 2nd Peter, the disciple sent a message of hope: joy and glory wait for all those who suffer for Jesus' sake.

Later, Peter himself was put to death on the cross by the emperor Nero.

Will God forgive all sin?

"If we confess our sins, He is faithful and just and will forgive us our sins and purify us from all unrighteousness." —I John 1:9

Who wrote the Book of Revelation?

The Church of Jesus Christ began to grow and spread throughout the world. As the years passed, there was only one person left alive who had walked the hills of Galilee with Jesus. The disciple John, now an old man, was a prisoner on the Greek island of Patmos. In this lonely barren place, God gave John glorious visions of the future, of the time when Christ would return to complete His work on earth.

Revelation is the only book of prophecy in the New Testament. It is filled with over 300 different symbols that tell about the future.

What does Alpha and Omega mean?

Alpha and Omega are the first and last letters of the Greek alphabet, like A and Z.

These letters are used as names for God in the book of Revelation. God is the first, the source of all creation, and He is the last, standing at the end of time. All that began in the book of Genesis comes to a conclusion in Revelation. In Genesis Satan and sin begin their rule over man. In Revelation Satan is destroyed for all time and sin is no more.

What is the Great Tribulation?

In his vision of the return of Christ, John saw a time of incredible human suffering and tribulation. As bad as other periods of history have been, they are nothing compared to what will come. Some day, the forces of evil that have been held back will be turned loose. John saw them as four horsemen, riding through the world spreading war, disease, hunger and death. People will run from the cities to hide in caves. They will pray for death, for at last they will fear the anger of God. During this Great Tribulation, many people will come to believe in Christ.

What is Armageddon?

In the Book of Revelation, the place where the kings of the world gather for the final battle between the forces of good and evil is called Armageddon. The Scripture promises that as the forces faithful to God face defeat in attacks from all side, Jesus Himself will return to wipe out the enemy and save His people.

What is the Millennium?

After the battle of Armageddon, Jesus, the Prince of Peace, will rule the earth for a thousand years, and people will understand at last how God intended life on earth to be - no war, no pain, no wild animals, no death. At the end of this time, Satan will be set free and he will gather the people for one last battle against God. Before that can happen, fire will destroy Satan's troops and Satan himself thrown into a lake of fire.

Then the final judgment time will come, when all people stand before the great white throne. The book of life will be opened, and each person will be judged according to what is written there.

Did John look forward to the return of Jesus?

John's vision ended with a view of the glorious new heaven and the new earth, prepared for those whose names were written in the book of life. An angel carried John to a mountaintop, and he watched the new Jerusalem coming down from heaven, shining like a jewel. The walls were made of precious stone and the buildings were gold. The city did not need a sun or a moon, for it shone day and night with the glory of the Lord.

In this vision of the final days, Jesus told John, "I am coming soon!"

John answered, "Even so, come, Lord Jesus!"